Treasure in the Field
Salvation in the Bible and in Our Lives

Robert A. Krieg

A Michael Glazier Book

LITURGICAL PRESS
Collegeville, Minnesota

www.litpress.org

A Michael Glazier Book published by Liturgical Press

Cover design by Jodi Hendrickson. Cover image: Thinkstock.

Excerpts from documents of the Second Vatican Council are from *Vatican Council II: The Basic Sixteen Documents,* by Austin Flannery, OP, © 1996 (Costello Publishing Company, Inc.). Used with permission.

1	2	3	4	5	6	7	8	9

Library of Congress Cataloging-in-Publication Data

Krieg, Robert Anthony, 1946–
    Treasure in the field : salvation in the Bible and in our lives / Robert A. Krieg.
        p. cm.
    "A Michael Glazier book."
    Includes index.
    ISBN 978-0-8146-8068-1 — ISBN 978-0-8146-8093-3 (e-book)
    1. Salvation—Biblical teaching.   2. Salvation—Christianity.
   3. Catholic Church—Doctrines.   I. Title.
BS680.S25K75   2012
234—dc23   2012040754

Contents

Preface

As we stood in a lodge overlooking the Grand Canyon, we listened to a park ranger explain how the canyon emerged over millions of years, where it extends today, and what plants and animals it now nurtures. The ranger advised us to walk at various points along the canyon's rim. If we did this, she noted, we would see the changing colors of its soil and stone, feel the air abruptly shift between hot and cold, and smell the fragrance of the shrubs and flowers. Our aim would be to know the Grand Canyon as well as to know about it.

Treasure in the Field has a similar aim. It is meant to heighten our awareness of God's love in our lives as well as to teach about the biblical witness to God's salvation. It invites us to experience anew Jesus' parable about the person who finds "treasure hidden in a field" (Matt 13:44). To what extent do we regard ourselves to be God's "treasure"? Further, to what degree do we live with the passion of someone who "in his joy . . . sells all that he has and buys that field"? While this book conveys information and ideas about the Bible, it also is written to promote fresh discoveries of God and of our true selves.

Given its aim, *Treasure in the Field* has four objectives. First, it discusses some of the Bible's classic texts, starting with Genesis 1 and ending with Revelation 22. In particular, it singles out biblical passages to which the church listens at Mass during the liturgical year.

Second, the book retrieves the Bible's teaching on salvation, also known as redemption. It studies the biblical understanding that God is "salvation" (Ps 27:1). To be saved is to meet the living God who delivers us from harm and leads us to the fullness of life, eventually beyond death.

Third, *Treasure in the Field* recasts the Bible's talk of salvation in contemporary terms. Since the word "salvation" comes from the Latin word *salus*, meaning "health," "wellness," and "well-being," the book defines salvation as God's gift of wellness, of our personal wholeness.

In this perspective, God calls us not to invent ourselves but to discover ourselves as God envisions us. As we find and accept ourselves as God's treasure, we are increasingly grateful to God, and, out of gratitude, we live the two great "laws": love of God and love of neighbor (Mark 12:28-34).

Fourth, this study undertakes a critical yet respectful approach to the Bible. It embraces the teaching of the Second Vatican Council (1962–65) in its Dogmatic Constitution on Divine Revelation, *Dei Verbum* (November 18, 1965): "Seeing that, in sacred scripture, God speaks through human beings in human fashion, it follows that the interpreters of sacred scripture . . . should carefully search out the meaning which the sacred writers had in mind, that meaning which God thought well to manifest through the medium of their words" (DV 12).

How should we "search out the meaning" of a biblical text? Building on *Dei Verbum*, the Pontifical Biblical Commission has provided its instruction, *The Interpretation of the Bible in the Church* (1993). First, according to the commission, we should clarify a text's "literal sense," that is, "that which has been expressed directly by the inspired human authors" (II.B.1). To determine this meaning we critically study a text in relation to its writer(s) or source(s), its historical and cultural settings, and its literary genre and literary features. Second, we elucidate the text's "spiritual sense" or "fuller sense," that is, "the meaning expressed by the biblical texts when read, under the influence of the Holy Spirit, in the context of the paschal mystery of Christ and of the new life that flows from it" (II.B.2). This second step sheds light on what *Dei Verbum* calls the Bible's "eternal wisdom" (DV 13). In other words, it clarifies the text's message for God's people today.[1]

Treasure in the Field highlights both the literal sense and the spiritual sense of biblical texts. Toward the former, it discusses each text's source, its historical and cultural context, and its literary aspects. Toward a text's spiritual sense, it elucidates the theological significance of Scripture in relation to our lives. In this endeavor, it is influenced by Carl Jung's study of our imagination and dreams. Moreover, it draws on the writings of Thomas Merton, OCSO, and also of Romano Guardini and his "students": Hans Urs von Balthasar, Karl Rahner, and Joseph Ratzinger, now Pope Benedict XVI. Exploring the literal sense and the spiritual sense of biblical texts, this book is meant to facilitate the kind of study of the Bible that "becomes a dialogue between God and the human reader" (DV 25).

Treasure in the Field relies on the metaphor that God is the gift giver who, having created us, now offers us salvation, *salus*. At the same time, God invites us to say yes to God's gift of our true selves. However, our response to this divine offer is often ambiguous. Either we do not seek our God-given personal identity or we do not embrace the personal identity that we have received. Moreover, not wanting to be vulnerable, we allow fear and suspicion to warp our relating to God and hence also to ourselves, other people, and creation. We must undergo a rebirth or *metanoia* in which we receive ourselves as God's treasure. However, we cannot undergo this change on our own. We need the advice and encouragement of other people as well as God's grace or love for us in Jesus Christ through the Holy Spirit (Rom 8:39; 2 Cor 13:13).

Jesus Christ is the Savior of all people, the bearer of God's liberating love. The Lord Jesus is the Word made flesh, the personal embodiment of God's complete gift of *salus*. At the same time, the Lord Jesus is the one human being who in the Holy Spirit sold everything and bought the field with its treasure, the treasure given by Abba, the Father. Thus, the crucified and risen Christ now guides and strengthens us through the Spirit to personal wholeness, to the kingdom of God.

Treasure in the Field includes no explanatory notes and a minimum of references to secondary literature. Commentary, study questions, and bibliography are available at http://www.nd.edu/~rkrieg. Scripture texts in this book are taken from the New Revised Standard Version (NRSV) of *The New Oxford Annotated Bible*, 3rd ed., edited by Michael D. Coogan (New York: Oxford University Press, 2001).

The author thanks the Liturgical Press's publisher Hans Christoffersen and its editors, Eric Christensen and Lauren L. Murphy, for their expert work on this book. He is grateful to the Louisville Institute for its generous research fellowship. He owes a debt of gratitude to the University of Notre Dame, most recently for granting him a research leave with financial support during the 2010–11 academic year.

This book has benefitted from many people's reflections on their journeys and on God. It is the fruit of teaching undergraduate students, beginning in 1975 at King's College (Wilkes-Barre, PA) and since 1977 at the University of Notre Dame. It has matured in response to young people's searching faith, honest questions, and fresh insights into God's saving presence and actions in our lives. Outstanding among these highly motivated learners was Elizabeth Mandile Borlik (November 2, 1973–May 2, 2009), who joyfully lived with a passion for truth and life.

Treasure in the Field has also emerged from the author's interactions with participants in adult education programs. He wishes to thank the Reverend James J. Bacik and the parishioners of Corpus Christi University Parish (Toledo, OH). He is also grateful to the participants in the workshops at The Oratory (Rock Hill, SC). With them, he remembers the gentle and wise Reverend David D. Valtierra, CO (July 11, 1947–May 21, 2010). Further, the author has prized his seminars with the Trappist monks of Mepkin Abbey (Moncks Corner, SC); he wishes to thank Abbot Stan Gumula, OCSO, and the Reverend Kevin Walsh, OCSO. Moreover, the author learned from the high school teachers and pastoral ministers in the National Catholic Educational Association's Word and Wisdom Symposium (June 2012), led by Kenneth L. Famulare and Thomas C. Cummings.

Drafts of this book received constructive criticisms from the author's colleagues Regina Coll, CSJ, and Lawrence S. Cunningham. Moreover, these drafts improved because of the recommendations of a new generation of theologians: Michael Anthony Abril, Kristin M. Colberg, Katherine F. Elliot, Brandon R. Peterson, Todd Walatka, and Jeffrey T. Wickes. Of course, the author alone is responsible for this book's content.

Many years ago, the Reverend Robert J. Kruse, CSC, at Stonehill College (North Easton, MA), enflamed the author's love for theological inquiry. At crucial junctures on the journey, Judith Anne Beattie, CSC, and the Reverend Frederick "Fritz" W. Pfotenhauer have offered wise counsel. The seed for this book was watered by Kathleen Cannon, OP, the Reverend Anthony "Tony" W. Gorman, OSB, and the Reverend Thomas F. O'Meara, OP. Most importantly, Elizabeth Fee Krieg has advised and inspired the author with her love, her inquiring spirit, and her sense of humor.

Treasure in the Field: Salvation in the Bible and in Our Lives is dedicated to Judith Krieg Stewart and David C. Stewart and also to Deborah Dacey Krieg and Peter C. Krieg. "How very good and pleasant it is when kindred live together in unity!" (Ps 133:1).

Chapter 1

God's Gift
Creation and Salvation

According to the Trappist monk Thomas Merton, there exists a widespread misunderstanding of "the beautiful Christian metaphor 'salvation.'" It is often thought that salvation is God's reward to us in the next life for our efforts at being religious and ethical in this life. But this popular notion does not match the biblical understanding of salvation, also known as redemption. According to the Bible, salvation is God's gift that we can accept or reject. Having graciously created us, God offers each of us the gift of personal wholeness and awaits our acceptance of God's gift, our true selves. "The object of salvation," Merton writes, "is that which is unique, irreplaceable, incommunicable—that which is myself alone."[1] In other words, to be saved is to receive ourselves from God.

Merton compares our being saved with our finding a jewel on the ocean floor and then our working to recover this priceless, unique gem. At birth each of us is a diamond whom God has created. But God does not demand that someone accept the jewel that he or she is. God awaits our yes to ourselves as God intends us. To accept oneself as envisioned by God is to allow oneself to be "drawn up [by God] like a jewel from the bottom of the sea, rescued from confusion, from indistinction, from immersion in the common, the nondescript, the trivial, the sordid, the evanescent."

Our task in life is, therefore, to embrace ourselves as God's treasure. Our goal is not to invent ourselves but to discover ourselves as we mature into the whole persons whom God has desired since our conception. According to Merton, our saying yes to ourselves as God

1

envisions us is what is often called "working out our salvation." For this reason, the Trappist monk advised: "Pray for your own discovery."[2]

Merton's view of salvation has its roots in the Bible. According to Jesus Christ, our welcoming salvation—which he called the "kingdom of God"—is similar to someone finding a "treasure hidden in a field" and then selling everything and buying that field. Further, saying yes to God's gift is like "finding one pearl of great value" and then giving up everything else in order to buy this one pearl (Matt 13:44-46). Each parable highlights both "finding" and "buying," both our discovering God's gift and our accepting this divine gift.

Jesus did not originate this understanding of salvation. Rather, he drew it from the Scriptures, the Hebrew Bible, which Christians call the Old Testament, the "first covenant." As Jesus knew, according to the book of Genesis, God called Abram and Sarai at Haran (in today's Turkey). Accepting God's call or gift, Abram and Sarai went forth to "the land of Canaan" (Gen 12:1-6). During this journey, they said yes to God's covenant with them, to God's promise to care for them and their descendants. Receiving God's love, they attained their personal identities as Abraham and Sarah (15:1-21; 17:1-27).

God's call or gift did not end with the biblical "patriarchs," namely, with Abraham, Isaac, and Jacob. Rather, God continues to reach out to human beings. According to the book of Proverbs, God offers us "Wisdom" and urges that we "not forsake her." If we heed Wisdom, "she will keep you; love her, and she will guard you" (Prov 4:6). In other words, as we listen to Wisdom or God's Word, we will discover our true selves and the path to the fullness of life.

But how do we know whether we are heeding Wisdom? By what criteria can we judge whether we are receiving ourselves as God's treasure in the field, as God's diamonds to be raised up from the ocean floor?

One answer to this question is available in biblical accounts of God's act of creation, of which the two most important are Genesis 2:4b-25 and Genesis 1:1–2:4a. These texts convey the understanding that our personal existence possesses basic qualities that God asks us to develop during our lives—our journeys that through God's grace can continue beyond death into eternal life. There are, to be sure, many human persons who face great difficulties—even insurmountable ones—as they seek personal wholeness in this life. Nevertheless, in the ideal, each of us as a diamond possesses these potential facets: to be a human person is to be an embodied, temporal, intelligent, and free individual who is an "I," a "we," and a "doer." After illumining these personal characteristics as conveyed in two biblical texts, we shall consider that God is the divine "I," "we," and "doer." It is therefore in God's "image" that we are created (Gen 1:26).

I. Genesis 2:4b-25, J's Account of Creation

Genesis opens with two distinct, though complementary, accounts of creation: Genesis 1:1–2:4a and Genesis 2:4b-25. Since the second text is the more ancient of the two, we will start with it. It tells of God transforming a desert into God's garden of "delight" (*eden* in Hebrew).

A. The Story of God, the Master Gardener

When "the LORD God made the earth and the heavens," there initially was a desert, an arid land with "no plant of the field" and "no herb of the field." However, "a stream would rise from the earth" (Gen 2:4b-6). The LORD God made the human person (*adam*) out of "dust" (*adamah* in Hebrew) and "breathed into his nostrils the breath of life." Next, "the LORD God planted a garden in Eden," and "there he put the man" in order "to till it and keep it" (2:8, 15). The LORD God told the human: "You may freely eat of every tree of the garden; but of the tree of the knowledge of good and evil you shall not eat" (2:16-17a).

Soon the LORD God observed, "It is not good that the man should be alone; I will make him a helper as his partner" (Gen 2:18). So God created various kinds of animals and brought them to the human person "to see what he would call them." The human named the creatures, "but for the man there was not found a helper as his partner" (2:20). So the LORD God put the human to sleep and removed a rib. "The rib that the LORD God had taken from the man he made into a woman" (2:22). When the man awoke, he met the woman and immediately said, "This at last is bone of my bones and flesh of my flesh; this one shall be called Woman" (2:23). Ever since then, "a man . . . clings to his wife, and they become one flesh" (2:24). "And the man and his wife were both naked, and were not ashamed" (2: 25).

B. The Source, Context, and Literary Elements of Genesis 2:4b-25

At this point, it is necessary to acknowledge the text's source, historical context, and some of its literary aspects. Genesis 2:4b-25 originated in Jerusalem from J, the abbreviated name of the Jahwist/Yahwist source. J was likely a group of scribes who worked in the mid-900s BC as King David and King Solomon were transforming Israel's confederacy of twelve tribes into a monarchy. J's creation account runs from Genesis 2:4b to Genesis 4:26. It recounts not only God's creation of the man and the woman in the garden but also the disobedience of the man and the woman, the birth of their sons Cain and Abel, Cain's killing of Abel, Cain's settling in "the land of Nod, east of Eden" (Gen 4:16), the birth of Cain's descendants, and the birth of Seth to Adam and Eve (4:25). This unit ends with the statement "At that time people began to invoke the name of the LORD," that is, the name Yahweh (4:26b).

J's account evinces to some degree J's historical situation. In telling of God creating the garden, J implicitly endorses the agrarian culture that David and Solomon promoted in their semiarid region. J also mirrors the patriarchal society of the day by saying that a husband "shall rule over" a wife (Gen 3:16).

Further, J likely knew the creation accounts of Israel's Mesopotamian neighbors. According to the Atrahasis story, the gods created human beings to do the work that the gods themselves refused to do. According to the epic of Gilgamesh, a semidivine snake frustrated the human desire for eternal life, and the human awareness of being naked occurred as a result of sexual intercourse. Although J adopted elements from these accounts, J recasts them in light of Israel's religious beliefs. Thus, J holds that the LORD God intends that human beings work with God in the garden (Gen 2:15), that the "serpent" is not divine but a "wild animal" (3:1), and that sin involves our turning away from God (3:6-7).

In Genesis 2:4b-25, J is seemingly standing beside God at the dawn of time and observing God in action. From this vantage point, J tells the story of God transforming a desert into a garden, a farm. Like a master gardener, God nurtures everything in the garden of his delight, Eden. In a sense, God gets God's hands dirty fashioning the "dust" (*adamah*) into the human person (*adam*), whom God invites to be God's cogardener or cocreator. Since God envisions creation becoming a fruitful, coherent whole, God wants the same for *adam*. Thus, the LORD God states, "It is not good that the man [*adam*] should be alone." God works with the human person to find a suitable "partner" (Gen 2:18). As a result, the garden's most fruitful moment occurs when God forms a woman (*ishah*) from a man (*ish*), who declares: "This at last is bone of my bones and flesh of my flesh." The man has identified "his partner," and God respects this human decision. Henceforth, "a man leaves his father and his mother and clings to his wife, and they become one flesh" (2:23-24). Now, along with the garden's fruitful plants and animals, the husband and the wife become whole, "one flesh," and hence creative, bearing Cain and Abel (4:1-2).

Confusion exists today among some people concerning the literary genre of the Bible's creation accounts, especially of Genesis 2:4b–4:26 and Genesis 1:1–2:4a. These two specific texts are mythic or symbolic narratives, not scientific theories. They are stories meant to answer the religious questions of *why* God created us and *why* suffering and evil exist. In other words, these narratives shed light on God's intentions and God's relationship to creation; they contain truths about God and God's creativity in time and space. These symbolic narratives do not necessarily conflict with theories of evolution that are meant to answer *how* the universe came/comes about and *how* we can lessen suffering in the world. Given its proper question, science is directed to empirical or measureable causality, not divine intentionality. Science is taken beyond its methods and limits when it is used to argue for or against God's existence and God's intentions and actions in creation. Conversely, the Bible's creation accounts are misread when they are viewed as scientific explanations of creation.

In light of this clarification, let's consider some of the truths about human persons and about God that are contained in Genesis 2:4b-25.

C. J's Views of the Human Person and God

According to J, human persons stand out among all of God's creatures and enjoy a unique relationship with God. God formed *adam* out of *adamah* as God "breathed into his nostrils the breath of life" (Gen 2:7). That is, God enlivened the human person out of God's very being. Creating *adam* prior to the earth's vegetation and animals, God envisioned the human person being God's cogardener. Hence, God placed *adam* "in the garden of Eden to till it and keep it" (2:15), and God respected "that whatever the man called every living creature, that was its name" (2:19). God was not satisfied until the human person had a "partner" who is a true equal, a "helper" from "one of his ribs." Finally, God is delighted when the man (*ish*) and the woman (*ishah*) "become one flesh," and thus they are creative as the garden is fruitful.

As depicted in Genesis 2:4b-25, a human person possesses in principle at least seven facets.

1. Human persons are <u>embodied.</u> Because God "formed man from the dust of the ground," we are rooted in the earth. We are woven into the very fabric of creation. Indeed, we relate in and through our bodies to ourselves, other human persons, the earth, and God. In particular, God created us as sexual beings who can "become one flesh." Indeed, "in the garden," that is, in the ideal world, we would accept our sexuality as God intended. We would not be ashamed of our bodies (Gen 2:25). Also, we would not fear death (3:19).

At the same time, we are more than our bodies. After forming the human person "from the dust," God "breathed into his nostrils the breath of life; and the man [*adam*] became a living being" (Gen 2:7). In other words, God has given us God's breath or Spirit so that we have the potential to be relational, creative, and free beings similar to God. This personal dynamism manifests itself in the next six qualities.

2. Human <u>persons live in time.</u> We possess the potential to change, and our change occurs over time. We are God's works in progress. In Genesis 2, the human person moves from being alone to becoming whole through marital union: "A man leaves his father and his mother and clings to his wife, and they become one flesh." This "leaving" and "becoming" mean that human persons make journeys that can be re-counted in stories or histories. In a sense, therefore, to be a human person is to be a story.

3. Human persons are <u>capable of intelligence.</u> Among the creatures, we have the unique ability to take in and critically reflect on the events and world that impact us. After perceiving something, we are able to draw conclusions by recognizing recurring patterns (inductive reasoning) or applying logical formulas (deductive reasoning). Although some other animals are also able to recognize problems and devise clever solutions, humans are distinctively able to perceive, understand, judge, and act according to wisdom. For example, the human person (*adam*) is able to name God's creatures (Gen 2:20).

4. Human <u>persons are free,</u> and they are respected in their freedom <u>by God.</u> God does not choose the human person's partner. God stands back and waits for the human person (*adam*) to declare: "This at last is bone of my bones and flesh of my flesh" (Gen 2:23).

5. Human persons are <u>subjects, not objects.</u> That is, each of us possesses the potential to be an "I." An "I" is a subject, one who can relate to herself and refer to herself from her singular, privileged perspective. No one else can assume this perspective on this person. In Genesis 2,

God respects the human being as an "I" when God acknowledges the human's intelligence and freedom to name the plants and animals and to select "a suitable partner," as well as to obey or to disobey God's instruction concerning "the tree of the knowledge of good and evil" (Gen 2:17).

6. Human persons are interpersonal beings. Each of us is a "we," a social being. Each of us withers and dies when deprived of mutually enriching relationships with other men and women. In this regard, God recognizes that "it is not good that the man should be alone; I will make him a helper as his partner." Every human person yearns to say to his or her loved one(s), "You are my 'other'; you are 'bone of my bones and flesh of my flesh.'"

7. Human persons are self-agents, "doers." We desire to do things for the genuine well-being of ourselves, other people, and the earth. We want to contribute to our communities. Each of us has the potential to have intentions, make decisions, act on these intentions and decisions, and we are responsible for our words, choices, and actions. Our Creator entrusts us to be cogardeners. God settles us in the garden "to till it and keep it," and God leaves us free to make decisions, for good or ill, concerning God's plants and animals: "Whatever the man called each living creature, that was its name" (Gen 2:19). As self-agents, we are responsible for our choices.

Let's sum up. As depicted in Genesis 2:4b-25, to be a human person is to be an embodied, temporal, rational, and free being who is an "I," a "we," and a "doer." God desires that each of us develops these seven facets and integrates them into our personal identity as envisioned by God.

What does this self-realization involve? Many of us desire to reach a healthy acceptance of our bodies so that we are healed of our preoccupation with our appearance, our eating disorders, and our uneasiness with our sexuality. Further, we yearn for a fuller integration of our journeys, of our transitions from one chapter of our stories to a new chapter. We are also aware at times that we could develop our minds in new ways and could exercise our freedom with greater responsibility for ourselves, others, and the earth. Moreover, we sense that we would attain more personal depth and insight into life (a) if we would become more comfortable with listening to silence, with having times and places for solitude, and hence with our "inner" life; (b) if we would strengthen our ways of interrelating with other people, especially with family and friends; or (c) if we would take more initiative and assume more responsibility for our lives. In other words, each of us is called by God to mature into a whole person who is a subject, a social being, and a self-agent.

At this point, let's turn to J's depiction of God in Genesis 2: God is the master gardener who transforms the desert into God's garden of delight. In other words, God is the supreme personal being who cherishes the garden and even abides within it. In this vein, J tells us in Genesis 3:8 that the man and the woman "heard the sound of the Lord God walking in the garden at the time of the evening breeze." God is not an absentee land owner but an intimate companion of all human persons in the garden. Thus, God is immanent; God abides within, though apart from, creation. Living at the heart of the creation, though distinct from it, the Creator is continually creating and sustaining the cosmos.

God, our immanent Creator, manifests at least three personal traits.

1. God is the Lord God (Gen 2:4b). That is, God is Yahweh, or, in Hebrew, YHWH. In most English-language Bibles, the title Lord (in upper case letters) functions in place of the divine name Yahweh; according to Jewish teaching, God's name is so sacred that we should not speak or write this divine name. What does this name mean or signify? It likely comes from the verb "to be" in the sense of "to live," which in Hebrew is *hayah*. Hence, YHWH may mean "the One who causes [us] to be." In other words, the Lord is the Creator, life's Source and the Goal (the Alpha and the Omega in Greek). The Lord abides at the heart of creation and yet exists apart from creation. More will said about this sacred name in our discussion of God's revelation to Moses (Exod 3:1-15; 6:2-9); see chapter 3.

2. God is depicted with anthropomorphic or human-like qualities. For example, in order to enliven the human person, God "breathed into his nostrils"; God also "planted" the garden (Gen 2:7-8). Moreover, God did not wait for the human person to speak of feeling alone. Rather, God knew the human person's loneliness and said, "It is not good that the man should be alone." Thus, God initiated the search for a "partner" for *adam*. God's human-like image shows God's effort to relate to us and to encourage us to relate to God.

3. God acts through natural elements and natural causality. For example, God forms *adam* from *adamah* and nourishes the garden with the river and rain. Further, delighting when *adam* finds a "helper as his partner," God is present to the man and the woman as they care for one another and "become one flesh." In other words, according to

J, all genuine encounters between human persons are simultaneously encounters with God. In the words of Victor Hugo's novel/musical drama *Les Misérables*, to love another person is to see the face of God.

Although J's account in Genesis 2 consists of only twenty-two verses, it provides insights into the complexity—the mystery—of the human person and of God. It presents the human person as an embodied, temporal, intelligent, and free being who is a subject, a social being, and a self-agent. As such, each of us is God's singular diamond, God's unique treasure in the field. Moreover, God is the immanent Creator, the master gardener, who continually cultivates the garden and invites us to collaborate in this divine endeavor. Not surprisingly, because Genesis 2:4b-25 is a treasury of wisdom concerning us and God, it is a point of reference for Genesis 1:1–2:4a as well as for the Bible's other accounts of creation, such as Psalm 104, Job 38:1–41:34, and Proverbs 8:22-31. It suffices here to discuss only Genesis 1:1–2:4a.

II. Genesis 1:1–2:4a, P's Account of Creation

For a few centuries, J's account of creation circulated on its own among the Israelites. Then in about 500 BC, it was incorporated by religious leaders into the collection of texts that came to be called the Torah (Hebrew, "law") and eventually also the Pentateuch (Greek *penta*, "five," + *teuch*, "tools" or "books"). In this compilation, J's ancient narrative of God as the master gardener (Gen 2:4b-25) was placed after a relatively newer account of God's act of creation: the story of God as the theatrical/liturgical director (Gen 1:1–2:4a).

A. The Story of God, the Theatrical/Liturgical Director

At the outset "the earth was a formless void." It existed in chaos, surrounded by "the deep," the tumultuous waters that "darkness covered." Then the "wind from God swept over the face of the waters" (Gen 1:2). After the wind, perhaps identical with the Holy Spirit, calmed the chaos, the Creator fashioned creation as a director would build a theater or Jerusalem's temple. Arranging the heavens and the earth for the drama that would soon ensue, God worked in an orderly manner over six "days."

On the first day God said, "Let there be light," and it happened. Then God "separated the light from the darkness" (Gen 1:4). On the second day God said, "Let there be a dome" to "separate the waters from the waters" (1:6). Thus, sky came between the clouds of rain and the vast ocean. On the third day God said, "Let the waters under the sky be gathered together into one place, and let the dry land appear" (1:9). This happened. God called the dry land "earth" and the waters "seas." Then "God saw that it was good" (1:10). God also said, "Let the earth put forth vegetation." This happened. "And God saw that it was good" (1:12).

On the fourth day God said, "Let there be lights in the dome of the sky to separate the day from the night" (Gen 1:14a). Thus the sun and the moon came about. Once again, "God saw that it was good" (1:18). On the fifth day God said, "Let the waters bring forth swarms of living creatures [e.g., fish], and let birds fly above the earth across the dome of the sky" (1:20). All of this happened. "God blessed them, saying, 'Be fruitful and multiply and fill the waters in the seas, and let birds multiply on the earth'" (1:22). Again, "God saw that it was good" (1:21).

On the sixth day God said, "Let the earth bring forth living creatures of every kind: cattle and creeping things [e.g., insects] and wild animals of the earth of every kind" (Gen 1:24). This took place, and "God saw that it was good" (1:25). God then said, "Let us make humankind in our image, according to our likeness; and let them have dominion over the fish of the sea, and over the birds of the air, and over the cattle, and over all the wild animals of the earth, and over every creeping thing that creeps upon the earth" (1:26). God bestowed a blessing and a command upon human persons: "Be fruitful and multiply, and fill the earth and subdue it" (1:28). Standing back, "God saw everything that he had made, and indeed, it was very good" (1:31).

By the seventh day, God's work was finished (Gen 2:1). God "rested on the seventh day from all the work that he had done." In resting, the Creator "blessed the seventh day and hallowed it" (2:2-3). Thus, there is now the Sabbath (Hebrew, "rest").

B. *The Source, Context, and Literary Elements of Genesis 1:1–2:4a*

The Bible's opening narrative was fashioned by P, the Priestly source, who worked during the sixth century BC. This group of writers likely originated in Jerusalem but during the exile resided in Babylon (today's Iraq); they returned to Jerusalem in 538 BC. In Babylon, P and the

Israelites differentiated themselves from their captors by stressing the religious beliefs and rituals that secured their identity as the people of Israel. In particular, they upheld their monotheism—namely, their belief that God abides above all other beings—and also their ritual of observing the Sabbath. P stresses these identifying features in the creation account.

P knew the Babylonian creation myth, the *Enuma Elish*, according to which the earth took shape as the result of a battle between the storm god, Marduk, and the goddess of the salt waters, Tiamet. This naturalistic view of divinity was rejected by the Israelites in general and by P in particular. Wanting to uphold Israel's view of God, P crafted a creation account with an emphasis on God's transcendence or otherness in relation to the cosmos. In effect, P not only opposed the *Enuma Elish* but also complemented J's creation account with its stress on God's immanence. According to P, God stands apart from "the heavens and the earth," and the "wind from God swept over the face of the waters" (Gen 1-2). In other words, abiding outside of creation, God sends the Spirit over the chaos. Moreover, God speaks the divine Word, which then shapes the cosmos: "God said, 'Let there be light'; and there was light" (1:3).

In Genesis 1:1–2:4a, P seemly watches God transform earth's "formless void" and "darkness" into an ordered realm filled with light. As noted earlier, P depicts God as the director of a theater or of Jerusalem's temple. In an ordered sequence, God arranges the space and then assembles the actors or players in it. God accomplishes a specific task on each day of work. On the first, second, and third days, God fashions the three arenas: the sky, the seas, and the earth. On the fourth, fifth, and sixth days, God creates the actors for each arena: the sun and moon in the sky, the fish in the seas, and the cattle, wild animals, and humankind on the earth. At each stage, God observes that the results of this labor are "good" (Gen 1:4, 10, 12, 18, 21, 25). When the sixth day ends, God sees that all of creation is "very good" (1:31). On the seventh day, God "rests"; God obeys the third commandment: "Remember the sabbath day, and keep it holy" (Exod 20:8). Soon the sacred drama of creation and history will begin.

Similar to J's creation story (Gen 2:4b-25), P's narrative (Gen 1:1–2:4a) is highly symbolic or mythical. Addressing the question "Why did God create us?" it illumines both God's gracious intention at the dawn of time and God's continuing care of creation.

P also highlights aspects of human life that J did not discuss. As previously noted, J holds that God's act of creation reaches its high point when the man (*ish*) and the woman (*ishah*) "become one flesh" (Gen 2:24). In other words, we meet God as we move in a horizontal direction, as we relate appropriately to ourselves, one another, and the earth. However, P teaches that God's act of creation culminates on the Sabbath, and thus we meet God as we, imitating God, "rest" on the seventh day of each week (2:3). While P affirms the God-given goodness of creation, P also maintains that we must move not only in a horizontal direction toward ourselves, one another, the earth, and the immanent God but also in a vertical orientation toward the transcendent God.

C. *P's Views of the Human Person and God*

Presupposing J's view of our personal existence as well as J's sense of God, P also accentuates our potential for self-transcendence and our reliance on symbols and rituals. P even links these human dimensions to God's qualities. We'll start with P's view of us as God's treasure and then take up P's view of God.

1. Although J recounts that God created *adam*, then the garden, and finally the woman and the man, P teaches that God's last and most significant act of creation occurred when God created us "male and female"—both together at one and the same time. Indeed, God has made us in God's "image," in God's "likeness" (Gen 1:26-27). What does this mean?

Building on J's view of the human person as a subject, a social being, and a self-agent, P accentuates our ability for self-transcendence. That is, we are capable of (a) becoming increasingly conscious of ourselves as subjects, social beings, and self-agents, (b) coming to insights and new questions about our personal existence, and (c) evaluating ourselves in relation to God's will for us. Given this dynamism, each of us can mature as an "I," a "we," and a "doer." In light of our potential for self-transcendence, God declares, "Let them have dominion over the fish of the sea, and over the birds of the air, and over the cattle, and over all the wild animals of the earth, and over every creeping thing that creeps upon the earth" (Gen 1:26).

2. According to P, we express God's relationship to us and our commitment to God by means of symbols and rituals. As the hearers and

readers of Genesis 1:1–2:4a, we are drawn through our imaginations into the theatrical or liturgical sequence of God's six days of creation that conclude on the seventh day, the Sabbath. Entering into this event, we marvel at God's creative work and sing the recurring refrain "God saw that it was good." We perceive too that our lives should follow the recurring cycle of six workdays moving to the day of rest.

P's emphasis on symbols and rituals occurs not only in Genesis 1:1–2:4a. It is also evident later on when P teaches that God's covenant with Abraham includes the circumcising of the Israelites' male infants (Gen 17:10), that God requires Moses to raise his hand and his walking staff in a ritual so that the waters would open during the exodus (Exod 14:16), and that God gives rules on the making and the use of altars, candles, and vestments (25–28).

Why does P uphold the value of symbols and rituals? They orient us to the transcendent God and also to human life's transcendent dimensions such as truth, justice, and love. When we do not keep the Sabbath, we neglect our uniqueness, our likeness to God. We behave as though we are no different than "the cattle and the creeping things." Yet when we keep the Sabbath, we engage in self-transcendence and reap its fruits. That is, on the day of rest, we step back from our everyday lives, enjoy sleep, leisure, and worship, and find ourselves refreshed and renewed as subjects, social beings, and self-agents.

Moreover, P's depiction of the human person as self-transcending and as reliant on symbols and rituals is congruent with P's view of God.

1. According to P, God is transcendent, existing outside of space and time and hence beyond our comprehension. God shapes creation through God's "wind," or Spirit: "A wind from God swept over the face of the waters" (Gen 1:2). Further, God influences creation through God's Word. P repeatedly writes, "God said. . . . And it was so" (1:3, 6, 9, etc.). Standing apart from the actual forming of creation, God is the theatrical or liturgical director who directs an invisible stage crew of angelic beings: "God said, 'Let there be light'; and there was light" (1:3).

In Genesis 1:1–2:4a, P accentuates the divine transcendence by not mentioning God's name, Yahweh/LORD. According to P, God explicitly revealed the divine identity to Moses (Exod 6:2-9). Thus, in P's view, human beings on their own have only a tentative sense of God. We cannot attain a clear understanding of God, because God is the supreme "other" beyond our intellectual grasp. Crucial for our knowing God is God's self-disclosure to us.

2. Further, according to P, God communicates to us through symbols and rituals. Acknowledging creation's goodness (Gen 1:4, 10, 12, 18), God regards creation as a potential symbol or concrete manifestation of divine love. In other words, God can meet us in a sunset, in the Grand Canyon, and in the birth of a child. Moreover, God can also come to us in rituals. Indeed, God engages in rituals such as blessings. On the fifth day, "God blessed" the fish and the birds, and on the sixth day "God blessed" human beings. Finally, God keeps the ritual of observing the Sabbath.

P's emphasis on God's transcendence and on God's reliance on symbols and rituals enriches P's understanding of God. According to P, God is the supreme personal being who abides in three modes of divine personal existence.

First, God is the divine "I," the divine subject. As God brings about creation, God steps back from it at the end of each day, reflects on what has come about, and admires it. For example, after creating light, "God saw that the light was good." After separating the earth and the sea, "God saw that it was good." Thus, God engages in the self-reflection of the divine "I."

Second, God is the divine "we," the supreme social being. When God states, "Let us make humankind in our image, according to our likeness" (Gen 1:26), God enjoys an infinitely rich personal existence in the company of angelic beings. More significantly, God is the divine "we" in that God the Creator sends the "wind," which may imply the Holy Spirit, across the waters (1:2) and repeatedly speaks the divine Word (1:3). P's talk of the Creator, Spirit, and Word is a wellspring for the Christian understanding of the triune or tripersonal God (see chap. 8).

Finally, God is the divine "doer," the divine self-agent. God intends something and instantly accomplishes it. P repeatedly writes, "God said. . . . And it was so" (Gen 1:3, 6, 9, 11, 14, 20, 24, 26, 29).

In sum, P witnesses to God's infinitely rich personal existence. God is the divine subject, social being, and self-agent in relation to whom God has created each of us an "I," a "we," and a "doer." In P's words, "So God created humankind in his image, in the image of God he created them; male and female he created them" (Gen 1:27).

III. Mystery

When the creation narratives of J and P are approached properly, they can prompt us to wonder anew about ourselves and about God.

Indeed, they can increase our awareness of ourselves as mysteries and of God as the ultimate mystery.

Talk about a mystery usually refers to a suspense drama. This kind of mystery—a mystery or dilemma to be solved—occurs in the novels of Agatha Christie, Mary Higgins Clark, and John Grisham. But there is another kind of mystery. There are true mysteries, inexhaustible realities that we can never solve but can increasingly and fruitfully understand. Foremost among true mysteries are ourselves and God.

A true mystery is a complex, dynamic, and irreducible reality that we can increasingly know but never fully comprehend. It is a reality that is more than the sum of its parts, and, although we may cognitively grasp each of its parts, we cannot fully comprehend this reality as a whole. As I try to know myself, a friend, my family, or God, I am wrongly inclined to reduce this living reality to one personal trait or even to a few attributes or qualities. Yet a human person is more than his athletic ability, more than her musical talent, and surely more than his or her personal appearance. Also, my family is more than its economic status and its inner conflicts. Further, God is more than our images and ideas of God. Our knowledge of a true mystery requires that we relate to this whole, vibrant reality that we cannot fully comprehend or control. Thus, we relate appropriately to a true mystery when we experience awe and even bewilderment in this reality's presence. Before the mystery of oneself, for example, someone may join the psalmist in praising God: "It was you who formed my inward parts; you knit me together in my mother's womb. I praise you, for I am fearfully and wonderfully made. Wonderful are your works; that I know very well" (Ps 139:13-14).

In order to understand a human person and God, I must commit myself in respect, trust, and love to this living reality, this "other." I should approach this mystery as a true mystery, not as a puzzle or problem to be figured out. Also, the effort to know myself or another human person or God is self-involving; I cannot remain detached in my outreach to the other. Rather, I must be ready to let go of my preconceived notions and my inappropriate ways of relating if I want to know someone better.

Moreover, in order to know human persons as mysteries and God as the ultimate mystery, we must employ stories and narratives. As the philosopher Hannah Arendt observed in her book *The Human Condition*, if we wish to know someone, we must tell and retell this person's story.[3] Why? A story or a narrative can convey a sense of the whole, a sense of the coherence and unfolding of someone's life. In this, it expresses the person's identity.

To be sure, personal knowledge of a true mystery relies in part on the methods, data, and conclusions of the natural and social sciences. If I wish to know myself better, I should learn, for example, from biochemistry and genetics as well as from psychology and cultural anthropology. But I must not stop there. I must also recount my life story to various listeners (including professional counselors), inviting their critical questions, insights, and alternative perspectives on my life's journey. In like manner, if I wish to know someone better, I should make use of the natural and social sciences. Yet I must also allow the person to tell me the story of his or her life, and at the same time I must empathetically enter into this narrative so that I try to walk in that person's shoes. In sum, knowing everything about someone is not the same as knowing this person.

The Bible repeatedly attests to the fact that each human person is a true mystery and that God is the ultimate mystery. As we have seen, the creation accounts of J and P highlight the richness and complexity of our personal existence and simultaneously the incomprehensibility of God. These texts convey the understanding that each of us is an embodied, temporal, intelligent, and free being who is an "I," a "we," and a "doer." Further, P's account highlights our potential for self-transcendence and our reliance on symbols and rituals as we relate to ourselves and to God. In sum, Genesis 2:4b-25 and Genesis 1:1–2:4a communicate the respect for human persons acclaimed by the psalmist who sings to God, "You have made them a little lower than God, and crowned them with glory and honor" (Ps 8:5).

If every human person is a diamond or pearl beyond our full comprehension, then our Creator surely far surpasses our complete understanding. As presented by J and P, God dwells within creation and yet exists apart from it. The Source and the Goal of the cosmos is paradoxically both immanent and transcendent. Marveling at the ultimate mystery at the heart of creation, the psalmist exclaims, "How great are your works, O Lord! Your thoughts are very deep!" (Ps 92:5).

Further, J and P witness to the fact that God is personal existence par excellence. God is the divine subject, the divine social being, and the divine self-agent. As such, God has created each of us to become an "I," a "we," and a "doer" in the divine "image" or "likeness." For this reason, as someone matures as a personal subject, an interpersonal being, and a self-agent, this person can meet God anew through these facets of personal existence. When someone experiences himself as an "I" with an "inner," mysterious life, he may hear God's whisper in his interior stillness. In this, he is similar to the prophet Elijah, who met God in "a sound of sheer silence" (1 Kgs 19:12). Further, as this same person shares a meal with friends, he as a social being may sense God's presence in this community. In this, he is similar to Moses and the others who enjoyed a meal together on Mount Sinai in God's presence (Exod 24:9-11). Finally, this same person may exercise his self-agency as he serves meals in a soup kitchen, and in this activity he may sense that he is collaborating with God in caring for God's chosen people. Thus, he may have an inkling of what Abraham and Sarah experienced at the oaks of Mamre: they gave food and drink to three strangers who were in fact God (Gen 18:1-15).

As each of us becomes a subject, a social being, and a self-agent, we can become aware of our God-given personal identities in relation to the one true God. Thus, we may find ourselves praying the *Shema* of the Jewish people: "Hear [*Shema*], O Israel: The LORD is our God, the LORD alone. You shall love the LORD your God with all your heart, and with all your soul, and with all your might" (Deut 6:4-5). Further, as we who are Christians acknowledge ourselves to be true mysteries, we may more deliberately make the sign of the cross on ourselves with the words "In the name of the Father and of the Son and of the Holy Spirit" (Matt 28:19).

IV. Creation and Salvation

According to Thomas Merton, God's saving or salvific action involves a person's discovery and acceptance of his or her true personal identity. To be saved is to find oneself as God's treasure in the field and to cooperate with God in uncovering this diamond. This insight by Merton is the idea that we develop in this book's subsequent chapters. Before doing this, however, we must clarify the Christian notions of creation, salvation, and redemption.

Creation is God's freely chosen, gracious act of bringing about the universe (out of nothing) and sustaining it. It is God's manifestation in time and space of God's selfless love, *agape* in Greek (Isa 43:7). It is God's garden of delight (Gen 2:4b-25), God's theater or temple for the drama of salvation (Gen 1:1–2:4a). As God's uniquely created beings, human persons are made in God's "image," God's "likeness" (Gen 1:26). As such, each of us is God's treasure, "crowned with glory and honor" (Ps 8:5).

The word "salvation" comes from the Latin *salus*, meaning "health," "well-being," "being whole." Hence, in Christian discourse, to be saved is to be made whole, to be empowered and guided in Jesus Christ through the Holy Spirit to become the person whom God intends. Salvation is therefore both a journey and a destination. It is both the process of receiving God's *agape* and also the full realization of one's personal identity beyond death. In sum, salvation is God's gift of personal individuation—ultimately beyond death, meaninglessness, and evil—in union with God and in communion with oneself, other people, and creation.

According to Merton's metaphor, each of us is a treasure or diamond that should not remain hidden but should come into full light. Human persons are jewels that must be raised from the ocean floor. Or, finding ourselves as God's treasure in the field, we must be uncovered so that we can bring delight to the Creator and enrich other people and the earth. To use yet another image, each of us is similar to the moon as it waxes from darkness into full light in the night sky. We are called to become—in union with Jesus Christ through the Holy Spirit—complete, luminescent circles radiating God's *salus* in a world in search of truth and light.

A synonym for "salvation" is "redemption." The word "redemption" has emerged out of the Latin *redimere*, which means "to purchase," "to buy back," and "to ransom." To be redeemed, therefore, is to be purchased and released by God from whatever and whoever prevents or resists our maturation into the whole persons whom God intends. We cannot redeem ourselves, because we are held back by our constraints (e.g., intellectual limits), by our situations (e.g., financial needs), and by negative forces (e.g., self-doubt). In its precise Christian sense, redemption is the process or act by which Jesus Christ has ransomed us from death, meaninglessness, and evil so that we might enjoy the fullness of God's life and love.

In order to visualize even further what happens as we find and accept ourselves as God's gift of *salus*, consider one more metaphor. At birth, each of us is a potential choir as well as this choir's assistant director. Each of my potential talents is a member of my possible choir. If all of my talents could be realized and brought into harmony, I would become a unified choral group, a whole person. However, these individual talents/voices and the assembly of these voices await development. As the assistant choral director, I can facilitate this development. But at the same time, I must work closely with God, the primary director of my potential chorus. As I rely on God's grace, I can become my harmonious whole as God envisions me. The day may even come when I, with my chorus of talents, may be brought beyond death into the heavenly realm where I may join with the new creation's choir in singing thanks and praise to God (Rev 5:13).

But there's a dilemma: I am reluctant to discover and accept myself as God intends me. I am fearful about hearing God's Word within me and about trusting the Spirit's guidance and strength. I am afraid of how I might be changed by this encounter with the living God. I avoid reflecting on myself as an "I," a "we," and a "doer." In sum, I cannot accept that I am a mystery and that I must give myself into God's hands, praying, "The LORD is my light and my salvation; whom shall I fear?" (Ps 27:1).

As noted earlier, Thomas Merton's metaphor of a human person as God's jewel alludes to Jesus' parables of the treasure and the pearls (Matt 13:44-46). According to Jesus, as someone finds their God-given identity, that is, the "treasure hidden in a field," he or she rejoices and immediately "sells all that he has and buys that field." As someone finds the "pearl of great value," he or she gives up everything in order to cherish this jewel. Thus, Jesus exhorts his listeners to find and to accept themselves as God's treasure: "The time is fulfilled, and the kingdom of God has come near; repent, and believe in the good news" (Mark 1:15).

Now consider a second interpretation of the two parables. Could it be that they also tell of God's discovery of us? In this view, God finds us in the earth and "sells all that he has" in order to hold each of us as a "treasure" or as "one pearl of great value."

This second reading of Jesus' two parables about God's kingdom aligns with Jesus' parables concerning God. God is the shepherd who goes in search of the one lost sheep. "When he has found it, he lays it on his shoulders and rejoices" (Luke 15:5). God is the woman who sweeps her house, "searching carefully" for her lost coin. When she finds her coin, "she calls together her friends and neighbors, saying, 'Rejoice with me, for I have found the coin that I lost'" (15:9). Further, God is the father who kisses his errant child even before the son repents of his wrongdoing. Embracing the lost child, the father declares, "Let us eat and celebrate, for this son of mine was dead and is alive again" (15:23-24). According to these parables, God persistently searches for us, and, as a result, God also empowers us to search for God and our true selves.

Acknowledging this divine marvel, St. Irenaeus of Lyons observed, "The glory of God is the human person fully alive." Ought we not therefore to live more fully? Ought we not to receive God's salvation, our very selves, so that we meet the living God and simultaneously become God's treasure giving glory to God?

Chapter 2

Sin
Our No to God's Gift

Imagine this scene. We are walking on a familiar path through a field on our way to a shopping plaza. As we chat about our recent activities, we're enjoying the warm sun and not thinking about the path we're following. But at some point we take a couple of steps off the path—perhaps because joggers are approaching or because an object in the grass catches our eye. In any case, we step to the side and suddenly sense the ground giving way beneath us. We fall, tumbling down a hole as though in a film such as *Indiana Jones and the Temple of Doom* or *Alice in Wonderland*.

When we hit bottom, we find ourselves on our backs and covered with dirt. Lifting our heads, we see in the dim light that we've fallen into an abandoned well or mine shaft. Above us is the opening through which we fell. We stand up and walk around in the hole. It appears that there's no way for us to climb up to the opening on our own. We can make our way back to where we were only if someone comes along and lowers down a ladder. We try using our cell phones but get no reception in the pit. We're trapped unless someone rescues us.

This imaginary account is a metaphor for what we may undergo from time to time. Everything is going as we expect, but then things fall apart. It may be that we've lost our job, or that our parents have decided to get a divorce, or that someone close to us learns of her terminal illness, or that we've failed at something important to us. Also, things can fall apart when we leave one phase of our lives and enter a new one. For example, we can find ourselves disoriented as we move from high school to college, from living with our parents to living on our own, or upon separating from our spouse. Or we can also fall into a dark pit because of an addiction to alcohol, drugs, pornography, the internet, overeating, staying thin, or shopping. When the addiction demon overcomes us and we hit bottom, we may realize that we cannot rescue ourselves. We need the help of other people, especially of others who are recovering from the illness from which we are suffering.

In all of these situations, after we fall from the path or routine with which we're familiar, we can find ourselves face to face with a basic, recurring question in human life: To whom do I turn for guidance and strength, especially when my life is in transition or seemingly in ruins? In other words, who is the primary author of my life story?

According to the Bible, God gives every human person the freedom to choose the primary authority for his or her life. God does not program us to accept God as our Source and our Goal, as the Alpha and the Omega. Rather, God gives us the space to choose for ourselves who or what will serve as our lives' compass and power, and we don't always choose God. As the Bible conveys, our inclination is to authorize other human persons, ourselves, or material things as our life's guide. In other words, we tend to make a finite reality into the god that controls our lives. Given our tendency to divinize a human person or an object, we are Adam and Eve rejecting the true God in favor of a god of our making.

Let's consider three forms of our exercise of human freedom and then employ these forms to analyze the story of "the Fall" of Adam and Eve and the story of Cain and Abel (Gen 3:1–4:16). Our inquiry into our use and abuse of human freedom will lead to a study of the fairy tale "Beauty and the Beast" and also of the Old Testament's book of Job. In conclusion, we shall define sin and reflect on Jesus Christ as the "New Adam," the God-Man who has established our appropriate exercise of human freedom.

I. Three Approaches to Personal Freedom

Time and again each of us faces a decision that requires the exercise of our personal freedom and thus manifests, to some degree, our stance toward God. Consider the imaginary situation of a high school senior named Ed who must decide what he will do after graduation. As Ed struggles with his decision, he could exercise his personal freedom in one of three ways.

fideism

Sin 23

One option is that Ed could allow other people to determine what he does. For example, he could simply follow the advice of his parents, who want him to study computer technology at the alma mater of his mom or dad. "Pick a school within our family!" But Ed is also being urged by his friends to go with them to the community college so that they can stick together. If Ed decides to rely uncritically on the directives of others, he is implicitly adopting an attitude called "heteronomy" (Greek *hetero*, "other," and *nomos*, "law"). He has in effect made other human beings his law, his authority. In its extreme form, heteronomy regards a human person or specific object as a god, an idol. Radical heteronomy occurs, for example, when someone is so infatuated with a friend that he or she blindly submits to the ideas and choices of this individual.

A second option in the exercise of personal freedom is that Ed could make a decision with little or no regard for the advice of parents, friends, and school counselors. He could opt to distance himself from everyone associated with him. If Ed were to assert himself in this manner, he would implicitly adopt a mentality called "autonomy" (Greek *auto*, "self," and *nomos*, "law"). In its extreme form, autonomy results in someone regarding himself or herself as a god, as the only authority for one's life. This attitude is expressed, for example, in Ayn Rand's novels *The Fountainhead* and *Atlas Shrugged*.

The third option is that Ed could make his decision about his life after high school by engaging in a threefold process of (1) considering the advice of others, especially the appropriate authorities, (2) taking seriously his own feelings, thoughts, and aspirations, and (3) listening to God's Word through the Spirit as known in his informed conscience. Conscience is crucial in this matter because, as the Second Vatican Council teaches, conscience is a person's "most secret core and sanctuary" where someone is "alone with God" (*Gaudium et Spes* 16). We acquire informed consciences by turning to God in prayer and by consulting various authorities both inside the church (e.g., pastors, teachers, the Bible, and church teachings) and outside the church (e.g., counselors, physicians, lawyers, and people known for their good judgment). If Ed were to make his decision on the basis of such a developed conscience, he would adopt an orientation called theonomy (Greek *theos*, "God," and *nomos*, "law").

Heteronomy, autonomy, and theonomy must be viewed, of course, in relation to the stages of our lives. For example, heteronomy is appropriate for babies and for persons with dementia. Also, autonomy is a developmental phase during our "terrible twos" and again during our early teens. Nevertheless, heteronomy and autonomy are problematic when they become deep seated and hence radical. As such, they put a human person where God alone should stand in dialogue with one's informed conscience.

Let's return to our opening scene of standing in a cold, dark place. In such a situation, radical heteronomy would dispose us to be passive, to wait for someone to resolve things for us. Trapped in an abandoned well, it would incline us to bemoan our fate instead of using our wits and energy to help ourselves. By contrast, radical autonomy would impel us to take charge of things and act rashly. It would dispose us to attempt the impossible, risking exhaustion and injury in our effort to dig or climb out of the hole. Note too that neither heteronomy nor autonomy would question our tendency to be preoccupied about ourselves. Indeed, they leave us thinking primarily of ourselves; they do not direct us to consider the well-being of the people who care about us.

Theonomy orients us to reflect and to pray as though everything depended on God and simultaneously to think, to judge, and to act as though everything depended on us in relationship with others. It directs us to undergo the decentering of our egos and the recentering of ourselves in God's Word through the Spirit. Simultaneously, it directs us outward to reflect, assess, and do something for our well-being and for the sake of the people whom we respect and love. If we were trapped in a pit, theonomy would orient us to pray that we would accept God's will, as Jesus did in the Garden of Gethsemane (Mark 14:32-42), and also to pray that God would care for our loved ones, as Jesus prayed at the Last Supper (John 17:11-24).

There is much at stake in how we exercise our personal freedom. Both heteronomy and autonomy can represent a refusal to accept one's life as God's gift. The individual who opts for radical heteronomy allows another human person or a human institution to determine his or her personal identity—the self that God alone should determine. The individual who chooses radical autonomy tries to invent his or her personal identity with no sense of being God's treasure. In both cases, the individual refuses to listen to the Word, Wisdom, speaking through the Spirit in his or her conscience. In sum, radical heteronomy and radical autonomy are denials of us as God's sons and daughters. By contrast, theonomy acknowledges creation's and hence our lives' Source and Goal. It orients us to acknowledge God to be the primary choral director with whom I, the assistant choral director, want to collaborate as I try to bring my numerous inner voices into harmony.

II. Genesis 3:1–4:16: Sin and Its Consequences

The story of the Fall of Adam and Eve is one of the Bible's best-known texts. However, it is also one of the Bible's most misunderstood texts. Genesis 3:1-24 makes no mention, for example, of an apple. In Latin the word for "apple tree" is *malus,* and the word for "evil" is *malum.* This similarity has led the Christian imagination to identify an apple tree, a *malus,* with the tree of forbidden "fruit" (Gen 3:2). However, in the text, the tree in question is "the tree of the knowledge of good and evil," the knowledge of *bonum* and *malum* (2:17; 3:5, 22). This ambiguity is indicative of other issues concerning Genesis 3:1-24. (There is no use, for instance, of the expression "original sin.") For this reason, we should follow the literary sense of this classic text. In particular, we shall note how Genesis 3 describes not a past event but the present reality that we often misuse our personal freedom as we relate to God, ourselves, other people, and the earth. As a result, we foster unhealthy relationships and dysfunctional interactions among people.

A. The Story of Us, of Adam and Eve, Rejecting God

The serpent "was more crafty than any other wild animal that the Lord God had made" (Gen 3:1). Thus, it set out to trick the woman in the garden. Whereas God had given permission to eat from every tree except one (2:16-17), the serpent twisted God's words as it asked, "Did God say, 'You shall not eat from any tree in the garden'?" (3:1). She correctly answered that God instructed her and the man to eat from every tree except "the tree that is in the middle of the garden." But she wrongly added "nor shall you touch it" (3:3). Further, God had said that if they ate from this one tree, they would "die," that is, they would put themselves outside the garden of God's *eden.* Challenging God's words, the serpent declared that if they ate from the tree, they would not die but would "be like God, knowing good and evil" (3:5). The woman saw that the tree gave good fruit, was beautiful, and was "to be desired to make one wise." Then the woman and the man ate the tree's fruit. At this, "the eyes of both were opened." Seeing "they were naked," they "made loincloths for themselves" (3:7).

In the evening, when the man and the woman heard the LORD God "walking in the garden," they hid among the trees. But the LORD God called, "Where are you?" The man answered, "I was afraid, because I was naked; and I hid myself" (Gen3:10). God asked, "Who told you that you were naked? Have you eaten from the tree of which I commanded you not to eat?" Disclaiming responsibility, the man answered that the woman "gave me fruit from the tree, and I ate" (3:12). The LORD God asked the woman, "What is this that you have done?" She answered, "The serpent tricked me, and I ate" (3:13). Thus she also denied responsibility for the deed.

At this point, God described the disobedience's consequences. To the serpent God said, "Upon your belly you shall go, and dust you shall eat. . . . I will put enmity between you and the woman, and between your offspring and hers" (Gen 3:14-15). To the woman God said, "I will greatly increase your pangs in childbearing," and your husband "shall rule over you" (3:16-17). To the man God said, "Cursed is the ground because of you; in toil you shall eat of it all the days of your life. . . . You are dust, and to dust you shall return" (3:17-19).

When God finished, the man "named his wife Eve," which means "life bearer" in Hebrew. Then God "made garments of skins for the man and for his wife, and clothed them" (Gen 3:21), and God sent them "forth from the garden of Eden, to till the ground," the *adamah* from which God had made *adam*, the human person (3:23). Finally, God placed cherubim at the edge of the garden and "a sword flaming and turning to guard the way to the tree of life" (3:24).

Further, the disobedience of the man and the woman had consequences for their sons: Cain, "a tiller of the ground," and Abel, "a keeper of sheep" (Gen 4:2). Cain resented that "the LORD had regard for Abel and his offering" but "had no regard" for Cain and his offering. God advised Cain that if he did not act out his resentment, he would "be accepted" by God. But God also warned Cain that "sin is lurking at the door; its desire is for you, but you must master it" (4:7). Cain did not, however, resist sin. In the field, Cain "rose up against his brother Abel, and killed him" (4:8). Then the LORD asked Cain, "Where is your brother Abel?" to which Cain replied, "I do not know; am I my brother's keeper?" (4:9). God exclaimed, "What have you done? Listen; your brother's blood is crying out to me from the ground! And now you are cursed from the ground [*adamah*]. . . . When you till the ground, it will no longer yield to you its strength; you will be a fugitive and a wanderer on the earth" (4:10-12). Cain cried, "My punishment is greater than I can bear!" He added that since henceforth he would be "a wanderer and a fugitive," he would be vulnerable: "Anyone who meets me may kill me" (4:13-14). Not turning his back on Cain, God promised, "Whoever kills Cain will suffer a sevenfold vengeance" (4:15). Moreover, God blessed Cain with "a mark," thereby protecting him. Then "Cain went away from the presence of the LORD, and settled in the land of Nod, east of Eden" (4:16).

B. The Source, Context, and Literary Elements of Genesis 3:1–4:16

Genesis 3:1–4:16, the story of Adam and Eve's disobedience and of Cain's murder of Abel, is a continuation of Genesis 2:4b-25, the story of God's transformation of the desert into the Garden of Eden (see chap. 1). Originating from J, who worked in Jerusalem during the mid-900s BC, it is a mythical or symbolic narrative. That is, it was intended by J to answer why-questions such as, why do we dread death? Why is it difficult for us to sustain healthy interpersonal relationships? Why do we have to work? Why do we find ourselves at odds with the land and with the weather?

The answer in general, given in Genesis 3:1–4:16, is that our difficulties in relating to ourselves, to other people, and to the earth stem from sin. What is sin? According to J's story, it is our attempt to be "like God" (Gen 3:5), that is, to have the power to determine what is good and evil and hence to have divine rule over all aspects of life. According to Thomas Merton, sin is the pursuit of a "false self." It is the effort to be the "illusory person" whom "I want myself to be but who cannot exist, because God does not know anything about him."[1] As Genesis 3 conveys, sin—by us as individuals and as groups—has negative consequences for all aspects of our lives.

J's narrative of Adam and Eve's sin was influenced by J's historical context. J knew that Israel's neighboring peoples were engaging in fertility rites that went contrary to the Israelite view of how we should relate to God, one another, and our sexuality. Since eating forbidden fruit is a possible metaphor for sexual misconduct, J may be condemning fertility rites by describing the action of the man and the woman as the eating of the fruit from the one tree that God said was off limits (Gen 3:6). Further, J may have depicted Cain as a farmer and Abel as a herder (4:3-4) in order to highlight the dangers of Israel's change during the

900s BC from its nomadic society with the herding of goats and sheep to its new urban society, especially in Jerusalem, with its reliance on farming. In support of Israel's ancient nomadic way of life, J reports that God subsequently made Cain nomadic, "a wanderer" (4:14). Yet, likely drawing on a different oral tradition, J adds that Cain eventually built a city from which emerged Israel's higher culture (4:17-22).

While the serpent represented a deity in the Mesopotamian religions, it did not do so in Israelite belief. Nor did the serpent in Genesis 3 stand for Satan; it did not gain this allegorical significance in Jewish thought until the 300s BC (see Wis 2:24). According to J, the serpent is "more crafty than any other wild animal" (Gen 3:1). Hence, it represents our human tendency to be crafty or deceptive in our relationships. This dark urge can move us to lie or to tell partial truths. Thus, the snake wrongly states that God has forbidden the man and the woman to eat from "any tree in the garden" (3:1). The woman corrects the serpent's words when she states that God's command concerns only the one tree "that is in the middle of the garden." But she is deceptive or crafty when she adds that God said not to touch the tree (3:3). In sum, Genesis 3 describes our often unconscious drive to deceive ourselves and others when we want to have things our way, when we want to be "like God," setting our own norms for good and evil, for right and wrong.

Among ancient Israel's neighbors the image of a tree represented sexuality, fertility, and regeneration. Thus, it expressed the human yearning for unending life. However, the image of the tree functions differently in Genesis 2–3. First, it is explicitly linked not with fertility but with God's life (Gen 2:9; 3:22), which God wishes to share with humankind (3:24). Second, the image of the tree is also associated with "the knowledge of good and evil" (2:9, 17; 3:5, 22). It represents the ability to understand all aspects of creation and to govern them, but not necessarily according to God's norms. This potential to comprehend and to influence creation belongs to human beings, who possess the freedom either to use this potential as God intends or to abuse it.

Finally, the image of the tree likely expresses not two realities but one mysterious reality seen from two perspectives. This one tree stands "in the midst of the garden" (Gen 2:9), that is, "in the middle of the garden" (3:3). This location is significant. Imagine that each human person is God's Garden of Eden. As such, each of us has at the center of our being God's Word, Wisdom, which is "the tree of life" and "the tree of the knowledge of good and evil." As a bicycle wheel is held together by spokes that radiate out from the wheel's hub, each of us has within us a center or unifying point where we meet God's Word, Wisdom, in the Spirit. This center point, a person's conscience, is meant to hold together and bring into appropriate relation all of someone's aspirations, talents, and limitations so that this individual over time moves toward his or her God-given personal identity. It is in this sacred space that God speaks someone's name and calls the individual to make a journey of faith as Abraham and Sarah did (Gen 12).

However, we—who are Adam and Eve—are continually tempted to disrespect our true center, "to eat" from "the tree of the knowledge of good and evil" in an effort to take control over it. In other words, we are inclined to impose our egos upon our lives, thereby displacing God's Word, Wisdom, at the core of our being. Why would we try to do this? We possess the urge to be "like God" (Gen 3:5). That is, we possess the impulse to determine our own identity so that we live in radical autonomy and also the impulse to authorize someone else or something else to define us so that we adopt radical heteronomy. In both cases, we reject theonomy, a life oriented to God's Word, Wisdom, abiding within us as the sacred tree "in the middle of the garden."

C. J's Views of Our Sinful Condition and of God's Love

Genesis 3:14–4:16 develops further the depictions of human beings and of God that J introduced in Genesis 2:1-24. It highlights how sin disrupts our personal existence, and this text simultaneously stresses God's unconditional love for us.

As a result of sin, we are not at home in our own bodies: "They knew that they were naked" (Gen 3:7, 10). We are also at odds with ourselves, with our crafty or sneaky wills (3:14). Further, we are estranged from the earth—"In toil you shall eat of it"—and thus we dread our return to the earth in death (3:17, 19). Also, we experience the earth to be "cursed," even though God has not in fact cursed it or us (3:14, 17; 4:11). We find it difficult to integrate ourselves as an "I," a "we," and a self-agent. We resist becoming more aware of our bodies, emotions, aspirations, and character strengths and flaws; the man's words are ours: "I was afraid," and "I hid myself" (3:10). Further, we try to control other people. No longer respecting the woman as "his partner" (2:18), the man "shall rule over" the woman (3:16). Siblings are rivals; Cain kills his brother. Denying responsibility for our actions, we blame others, especially our loved ones (3:12-13). We also feign ignorance of the impact of our actions. With Cain, we exclaim, "I do not know; am I my brother's keeper?" (4:9). Thus, we waffle back and forth between radical heteronomy and radical autonomy, as we deceive ourselves about our sneaky wills and about our urge to be "like God."

Nevertheless, God does not turn away from us. While "walking in the garden," God desires to be with the man and the woman who have turned away from God. God calls to us: "Where are you?" (Gen 3:9). Similar to a loving parent with children, God invites Adam and Eve to tell the truth about what occurred: "Who told you that you were naked?" (3:11). Similarly, God later asks Cain to speak the truth: "Where is your brother Abel?" (4:9). But neither Adam and Eve nor Cain can bring themselves to admit what has occurred. They—and we—are disposed to self-deception. After God explains to Adam and Eve and also to Cain the negative consequences of their actions (3:14-19; 4:11-12), God assures them of God's merciful love. That is, making leather garments for Adam and Eve, God clothes them as a parent dresses children who are about go out into the snow (3:21). Later, God compassionately blesses Cain with "a mark," a pledge of God's continuing offer of *salus* (4:15). J's depictions of God's unswerving care for Adam, Eve, and Cain brings to mind Jesus' images of God as the shepherd retrieving a stray sheep, as the woman finding her lost coin, and as the father embracing his errant son (Luke 15:1-32).

What's the upshot of Genesis 3:1–4:16? J's imaginative description of our lives in relation to God's grace brings us face to face with questions of personal freedom: Why does God allow us to reject God? How are we living radical heteronomy, radical autonomy, or theonomy?

III. Freedom and Love in "Beauty and the Beast"

When we find ourselves or others sitting in a cold, dark hole, we may ask, why does God permit things to go awry? The biblical answer is this: love is possible only when there is the freedom not to love, and freedom is the wellspring for love and yet also for sin. Let us consider this twofold truth in general terms, then in the fairy tale "Beauty and the Beast," and finally in the book of Job.

Love and freedom are interdependent. If love is to exist between God and ourselves or among human beings, then this love must allow the possibility of one party or the other walking away from this relationship. Love cannot be forced or demanded. God permits Adam and Eve—and us—to reject God because God desires that Adam and Eve—and all of us—relate to God in love, grounded in trust and truth.

At the same time, personal freedom includes the ability and the decision to enter into and nurture interpersonal relationships. As we grow in true independence, we gain the maturity, the respect for personal boundaries, and the skills to commit ourselves to others in selfless love. According to J, God desires that Adam and Eve develop so that they will freely choose to trust God. Even after they sin, God remains intent on their flourishing in the world: "The LORD God made garments of skin for the man and for his wife, and clothed them" (Gen 3:21).

The interrelationship between freedom and love manifests itself in "Beauty and the Beast." The Beast, a self-absorbed prince, dwells alone in his castle and manipulates the creatures that serve him. He eventually imprisons an elderly man who mistakenly enters the castle. When Belle, the man's daughter, learns of her father's plight, she selflessly takes her father's place in the castle. In doing this, Belle puzzles the self-centered Beast. As Belle waits on the Beast, she unintentionally gains his attention. The Beast gradually takes an interest in Belle and even begins to respect her. As he increasingly awaits her brief visits with his meals, he is no longer completely turned in on himself. He senses his latent potential for loving another person.

When Belle hears that her father is gravely ill at home, she requests that the Beast temporarily free her. She promises him that she'll return after she's helped her father.

Having begun to respect and to care for Belle, the Beast faces a quandary. If he keeps Belle locked in the castle, he'll deny Belle the freedom to choose to respect and to care for him. Yet if the Beast allows Belle to leave the castle, he may lose her forever. Moving beyond his preoccupation with himself, the Beast takes the risk; he allows Belle to walk away from his castle. Without Belle, the Beast is lonely and sad; he pays a personal price for respecting Belle's freedom.

In her freedom, while assisting her father, Belle discovers her affection for the Beast. When she hears that the local bully is taking advantage of the people in the village, she thinks what was previously unthinkable: perhaps the self-absorbed Beast will help other people. She sends word to the Beast, who is struck by Belle's trust in him. He leaves his castle, goes to the village, deals with the bully, and then returns to his castle without demanding that Belle accompany him. Once again, the Beast has overcome his preoccupation with himself. When Belle's father regains his health, she chooses to return to the Beast. As she approaches the Beast, she releases the Beast's goodness and potential for love. In an instant, the Beast is transformed into his true identity: a selfless prince.

"Beauty and the Beast" expresses a twofold truth. Genuine love is possible only when someone is free not to love, and authentic independence enables someone to mature into a person capable of truly loving someone else. This truth applies not only to our relationships with one another but also to our relationship with God.

IV. The Book of Job: A Story of Freedom and Love

The book of Job is a literary masterpiece concerning the issue of God's relationship to human suffering. It is pertinent here because it views the Creator-creature relationship within the interpersonal dynamism of freedom and love.

A. The Original Folk Tale

The book of Job enlarges an ancient folk tale that is contained in the book's prologue and epilogue (Job 1:1–2:13; 42:7-17). In this ancient story, Job is a "blameless and upright" man for whom God has great affection. Indeed, God cares so much for Job that God protects him from harm. On one occasion when God consults the council of "heavenly beings" (1:6), God is asked about the special protection of Job. The question is posed by the heavenly being charged by God to serve as God's "accuser" or "adversary," as "Satan" (*ha-satan* in Hebrew). (It was not until the fifth century BC that Israelite thought understood Satan to be evil personified.)

In the divine council, Satan contends that if God loves Job, then God should allow Job to accept or to reject God as Job copes with life's hardships. Satan accuses God: "Does Job fear God for nothing? Have you not put a fence around him and his house and all that he has, on every side?" (Job 1:9-10). If Job is not free, then Job cannot choose to love God. Could it be that Job only loves God because of what God has given him? Not wanting to inhibit Job's freedom, God says to Satan, "Very well, all that he has is in your power" (1:12). After this, Satan brings disasters on Job's oxen and donkeys and then on his sons and daughters. Job is upset by what has befallen his herds and, more significantly, his family. However, he remains faithful to God, even declaring, "The LORD gave, and the LORD has taken away; blessed be the name of the LORD" (1:21).

During a subsequent divine council, God boasts to Satan that Job "still persists in his integrity" (Job 2:3). But Satan dares God, "Stretch out your hand now and touch his bone and his flesh, and he will curse you to your face." God responds, "Very well, he is in your power; only spare his life." So Satan afflicts Job with a serious skin infection. Pained by Job's illness, Job's wife tells him, "Curse God, and die." But still loving God, Job rhetorically asks, "Shall we receive the good at the hand of God, and not receive the bad?" (2:10).

At this point, the original folk tale jumps to its conclusion: "The LORD blessed the latter days of Job more than his beginning; and he had fourteen thousand sheep. . . . He also had seven sons and three daughters. . . . And Job died, old and full of days" (Job 42:12-17). The folk tale's message is clear: God will reward us if we remain faithful to God through bad times as well as through good times. "Shall we receive the good at the hand of God, and not receive the bad?" (2:10).

Beginning in the 700s BC or so, the original folk tale circulated among the Israelites and strengthened their faithfulness to God during their hardships. However, it also fueled a theology of divine retribution, which holds that God rewards us when we remain faithful to God, and God punishes us when we reject God. Moses himself allegedly espoused a theology of divine retribution: "If you obey the commandments of the LORD our God . . . , then you shall live. . . . But if your heart turns away and you do not hear, . . . you shall perish" (Deut 30:16-18; see chap. 4).

B. The Book's Author, Context, and Literary Elements

The book of Job expands the original folk tale from roughly three chapters into forty-two chapters. It includes three cycles of poetic speeches by Job and his friends Eliphaz, Bildad, and Zophar: Job 3:1–14:22; 15:1–21:34; and 22:1–28: 28. After the third cycle, there is a summary of Job's argument: Job 29:1–31:40. The next unit, inserted at a later date, contains the speeches by the latecomer Elihu: Job 32:1–37:34. Finally, the book reaches its high point: God's speeches and Job's response, Job 38:1–42:6.

Why did someone enlarge the original folk tale? The book of Job's author probably worked during the 400s in Jerusalem, where he opposed the theology of divine retribution that some religious leaders were promoting in the aftermath of the Babylonian exile. Beginning in the early 500s, Israelites who had moved from Babylon to Jerusalem were asking, Why did God allow or will the Babylonians' destruction of Jerusalem's temple in 586 BC and the enslavement of God's chosen people in Babylon? The answer is contained, some religious leaders held, in the theology of retribution: God had sent the Israelites into slavery in the late 500s because the Israelites had turned away from God during the 600s; after they repented during their captivity, God sent King Cyrus of Persia to liberate them in 538 BC.

The book of Job's author has transformed the original folk tale into an extended dialogue between the proponents of the theology of divine retribution and the proponents of a more sophisticated view of God's relationship to human suffering. On the one hand, Eliphaz, Bildad, Zophar, and Elihu argue that Job is suffering because he has somehow sinned against God. If Job would admit his sin and repent, he would receive God's blessing. Making this point, Eliphaz states, "How happy is the one whom God reproves; therefore do not despise the discipline of the Almighty" (Job 5:17). On the other hand, Job renounces the theology of retribution and demands that God give an explanation for human suffering. Job declares, "But I would speak to the Almighty, and I desire to argue my case with God" (13:3).

When God finally speaks, God chides Job for trying to grasp God's reasons for allowing human misery. God, "out of the whirlwind," admonishes Job, "Who is this that darkens counsel by words without knowledge? . . . Where were you when I laid the foundation of the earth?" (Job 38:2, 4). In other words, human beings can never completely understand God, the ultimate mystery. Having called attention to the infinite gap between God's "mind" and the human mind, God dismisses human efforts to give a theory of human suffering. Among these is the theology of retribution that Job's friends defended. Agreeing with Job, God tells Eliphaz that he and the others "have not spoken of me what is right, as my servant Job has" (42:7). According to the book of Job, God wants nothing to do with a theology of divine retribution.

C. *The Book's Views of God and Our Personal Existence*

The book of Job communicates both the view of God expressed in the original folk tale and its own adapted view of God. We'll take each in turn.

According to the original tale, God exists in a realm wholly separate from human affairs: God is transcendent. God is called LORD/ Yahweh in the sense of the transcendent God, not in the sense of the immanent God as presented in J's narrative of Adam and Eve (Gen 2:4b–4:16). Dwelling "above" history and surrounded by the heavenly court, God takes pride in God's people when they remain "blameless and upright" (1:8). For example, God is pleased when Job undertakes the appropriate religious rituals (1:4-5; 42:8-10). Although God does not send misery, God allows it to befall Job and us (1:11-12). Further, if we keep our faith in God during bad times as well as good times, God will eventually reward us for our faithfulness (42:10). Thus, as already noted, the tale concludes, "The LORD blessed the latter days of Job more than his beginning." Indeed, Job "saw his children, and his children's children, four generations. And Job died, old and full of days" (42:12, 16-17).

Now consider the complete book of Job's more complex view of God. Unlike the original tale in which God is called LORD/Yahweh (Job 1:6, 7) and Elohim, "God" or "gods" (1:8; 2:3), the book of Job uses other names as well: *El*, "God"; *Eloah*, "God"; and *Shaddai*, "the Almighty." Further, it conveys divine transcendence by implying that God patiently stands back and listens to the lengthy dialogues between Job and his interlocutors (3:1–37:24). Yet the book does not neglect divine immanence: it depicts God stepping into the drama and giving an impassioned speech to Job. Then, inviting Job's response, God says to Job, "Gird up your loins like a man" (38:3) and "Anyone who argues with God must respond" (40:2). Most importantly, God's speech conveys God's assurance that God knows Job's plight and that his suffering does indeed possess a meaning or significance that is beyond human understanding. In this vein, God asks: "Who is this that darkens counsel by words without knowledge?" (38:2). In other words, Job must trust God, even amid apparently senseless misery such as the Babylonian captivity.

Given its view that the human mind cannot understand God's relationship to our suffering, it is fitting that the book of Job builds to its protagonist's concluding words: "I know that you can do all things, and that no purpose of yours can be thwarted" (Job 42:1). Although these words do not match the message of the original tale, they express the complete book of Job's more sophisticated view that although we can never fathom the full significance of suffering, we can trust that God will keep God's pledge or covenant to bestow *salus* upon us.

D. Theonomy Generates Questions, Even Doubt

When the story of Adam and Eve's sin (Gen 3:1-24) and the book of Job are read side by side, as we've done, they show that humanity's sin occurs because of our misuse of the personal freedom that is a prerequisite for our love of God. If there were no possibility of us rejecting God, then there would also be no possibility of us accepting God. In other words, God is committed to our freely choosing God, even though this divine commitment means that God must find appropriate ways to deal with sin and evil in creation.

Something else is noteworthy. Genesis 3:1-24 and the book of Job convey the distinction between someone's turning away from God and someone's questioning God. The first stance toward God is sin, arising from radical heteronomy and radical autonomy, and the second stance toward God is love, arising from theonomy. Let's consider the second orientation, Job's faithfulness, after which we'll turn to Adam and Eve's sin.

The original folk tale tells that God has appointed a heavenly being to assume the role of the "accuser." In other words, God welcomes questions and even accusations from the "heavenly council" and, as we'll now see, also from human beings.

Picking up where the original tale leaves off, the book of Job develops the insight that Job receives God's praise for his tough questions to God. Although Job refused to "curse God" (Job 2:9), he "cursed the day of his birth" when he declared, "Let the day perish on which I was born. . . . Let that day be darkness! May God above not seek it, or light shine on it" (3:1-4). In other words, Job accuses God of making a mistake in bringing about Job's conception. Job also presses God to explain why an innocent person suffers: "When I looked for good, evil came; when I waited for light, darkness came" (30:26). Hearing nothing from God, he audaciously exclaims, "O that I had one to hear me! (Here is my signature! Let the Almighty answer me!) O, that I had the indictment written by my adversary!" (31:35).

Given its rich storyline, the book of Job manifests the complex character of theonomy. Unlike Adam and Eve, Job is not acting on humanity's dark urge to be "like God" (Gen 3:5). Rather, he is motivated to question God because of his genuine faith in God. Further, as Job poses his questions, complains to God, and engages in lamentation, Job opens himself to God's living Word (Job 38:1–41:34). At the end of this painful process, Job attests that his questioning of God has led him not away from God but into closer union with God. He attests, "I had [previously] heard of you by the hearing of the ear, but now my eye sees you" (42:5). By questioning God's wisdom, Job has disposed himself to an encounter with the living God.

In sum, Job represents the vibrant faith in God that generates questions, even questions concerning God's covenant with us. In this, Job is similar to religious figures in world literature and contemporary life. Consider, for example, Tevia in Joseph Stein's book and musical drama *Fiddler on the Roof*. Think too about Dr. Bernard Rieux in Albert Camus's novel *The Plague*. Further, compare Job with Elie Wiesel in his memoir *Night* and also with Mother Teresa of Calcutta in her posthumous book *Come Be My Light*. These creative works express faith-inspired questioning of God similar to the faith that generated the book of Job. According to Cardinal John Henry Newman, the path to God—theonomy—includes our questions to God and even our doubting of God's wisdom.[2]

V. Sin: Inventing a False Self

Let's retrace our steps. J's narrative of the Fall and the book of Job highlight a crucial issue in our lives: Who stands at the unifying point within me from which flow all aspects of my personal identity? Do I authorize another human being or an object to control my life (radical heteronomy)? Or do I impose my ego on the world (radical autonomy)? Or do I acknowledge that my true center is God's Word, Wisdom, in the Spirit (theonomy)? If the latter is the case, do I exercise Job's freedom to question God while remaining faithful to God?

Again, imagine that a human person consists of numerous voices or potential talents, each awaiting development in itself and also in relation to the person's other voices. The person herself must decide how to use her personal freedom. Opting for radical heteronomy, she will give the "task" of her individuation to someone else (e.g., to a parent or a friend) or to something else (e.g., to an addiction). Or, choosing radical autonomy, she will claim sole authority for her life. Or, electing theonomy, she will see herself as the assistant choir director committed to working closely with God, the primary choir director.

The issue of personal freedom runs through every day of our lives; it shapes how we relate to ourselves, other people, and the earth as well as to God. Insofar as I live out of a false center, I interact inappropriately with everyone and everything. I'm like a moving car that shakes because its front wheels are out of alignment. Yet to the degree that I am centered in God, I can enter into healthy relationships with myself, other people, and creation. The issue of freedom may come to our awareness when we find ourselves in a dark hole at an apparent dead end. In such a situation, we may ask ourselves whether we are living a false self, that is, a personal identity imposed on us by someone else or by ourselves. A transition or a crisis in our lives can challenge us to return to our innermost being where God's Word, Wisdom, awaits us.

Thomas Merton writes, "All sin starts from the assumption that my false self, the self that exists only in my egocentric desires, is the fundamental reality of life to which everything else in the universe is ordered." In contrast, salvation and hence my true personal existence come about as I allow the decentering of my ego and the recentering of myself in God. "Ultimately the only way that I can be myself is to become identified with Him in Whom is hidden the reason and fulfillment of my existence." Acceptance of God's gift of *salus* requires me to acknowledge that God alone stands at my center, "in the middle of the garden" (Gen 3:3). Time and again, I must approach the sacred space within me and listen anew to Wisdom in the Spirit speaking my name, my personal identity. When I do this, I shall find that "the secret of my identity is hidden in the love and mercy of God."[3]

VI. Jesus Christ, the New Adam

"Attitude is everything." This adage appears on a poster atop a bulletin board of a community college near our home. It attests that we must not only gain our knowledge, expertise, and skills (e.g., in accounting, computers, or nursing) but also adopt an upbeat or hopeful mind-set. If we carry a chip on our shoulder, we will not be an appealing job candidate or an amiable colleague. Further, if we lack self-confidence, we will likely disregard a possible job opening because we'll doubt our qualifications for it. In short, how we approach people and situations determines much of what we find and what unfolds for us.

This adage, "Attitude is everything," is pertinent when we are sitting in a cold, dark place at a dead end. At such a moment, if we are living in radical heteronomy or radical autonomy, we will likely slide into a self-defeating attitude. But if we embrace theonomy, then we'll place our hope not in other people or in ourselves but in God. We will trust that God will deliver us, that God will save us—through people from whom we didn't expect help, or through untapped resources within ourselves, or through a "coincidental" turn of events. To be sure, the day will come when each of us will face death. At this time, will we trust in God to lift us out of the pit into eternal life? Some of life's most intense religious experiences occur when our lives are in transition or in ruins. In these situations, we are most prone to take the first step of admitting, "I cannot help myself; I must rely on the 'Higher Power.'"

Moving from radical heteronomy or radical autonomy to theonomy is no easy transition. We resist this change because of our impulse to flee from God's Word and also because of today's emphasis on self-indulgence and narcissism. Allowing my ego to be decentered so that I will become increasingly centered in God seemingly requires that I swim against the undertow in myself and also against the tide in our society.

Jesus Christ through the Holy Spirit makes it possible for all people to move toward God and hence their true selves. Indeed, according to St. Paul, the Lord Jesus is the New Adam who has freed the human family from the sin of the first Adam. Writing in about AD 54 to the Christians at Corinth, Paul observed that "just as in Adam all die, so too in Christ shall all be brought to life" (1 Cor 15:21-22). Although at birth we are the children of Adam and Eve, possessing the urge to displace God from "the middle of the garden," we can undergo a spiritual or "second" birth in which we become united with "the last Adam," who "became a life-giving spirit" (1 Cor 15:45; cf. Rom 5:12-21).

Our change in attitude is ultimately possible because Jesus Christ himself lived in complete faithfulness to God. In his letter to the Christians at Philippi (AD 55), Paul stresses our theonomy in relation to Christ's life: "Let the same mind be in you that was in Christ Jesus" (Phil 2:5). What was this "mind" or attitude? Paul immediately quotes the ancient Christian hymn that Jesus "emptied himself," that he "humbled himself and became obedient to the point of death—even death on a cross." Contrary to Adam and Eve, who tried to be "like God" (Gen 3:5), Christ remained faithful to God and dedicated to God's people, even amid his absurd suffering and death on the cross. Through his faithfulness to God, the Lord Jesus overcame the immoveable obstacle or dark urge in the human family that has obstructed our union with God. Christ opened the way for us beyond evil, death, and meaninglessness to the fullness of salvation. He became the Savior: "God also highly exalted him and gave him the name that is above every name." Raised to eternal life, Jesus Christ now abides in the Spirit with the Father, and all creation "should confess that Jesus Christ is Lord, to the glory of God the Father" (Phil 2:6-11).

This hymn about Jesus Christ's self-emptying (*kenosis* in Greek) and exaltation has crucial significance for us when we live in theonomy. As we assume "the same mind . . . that was in Christ," we seek to hear anew God's Word, Wisdom, through the Spirit within us and in the situations in which we find ourselves. Even when we find ourselves in a cold, dark place, we can receive—as St. Paul states—our "own salvation with fear and trembling; for it is God who is at work in you, enabling you both to will and to work for his good pleasure" (Phil 2:12-13).

This short reflection on the New Adam anticipates chapters 6, 7, and 8 concerning Jesus Christ as God's Son and the Savior of all people. Before moving into that discussion, however, let's study what the Old Testament teaches about our rebirth or conversion into theonomy (chap. 3), about God and human suffering (chap. 4), and about hope in God (chap. 5).

Chapter 3

Conversion
Our Yes to God's Gift

Many of us see our lives as journeys. We envision ourselves on an adventure that began when we as children imagined our future, prepared to leave home, and set out in pursuit of our dreams. Similar to Dorothy in *The Wizard of Oz*, we feel both excitement and trepidation as we make our way forward. We take risks, weave our way through obstacles, and know both success and failure. We also meet traveling companions such as the tin man, the scarecrow, and the lion; we help them, and they us. Like Dorothy, we gain self-confidence as we proceed, forge strong ties with others, and act so that we can reach our goals. It gradually dawns on us that we do not need "the wizard of Oz." We've found that we can pursue our dreams without relying on magic.

Our view of our life journeys is often similar to and yet different from the biblical understanding of life as a journey. The Old Testament tells how Abraham and Sarah, Jacob, Moses, and Ruth left their homes, faced hardships, bonded with other people, and eventually settled where they were meant to be. The New Testament tells how Jesus left his home in Nazareth, ministered in Galilee and the surrounding regions, and proclaimed his message in Jerusalem. This biblical storyline is similar to one that may shape our life stories. However, the Bible's accounts may differ from ours in that they make explicit what we often leave implicit. The biblical narrators speak of God as the most important "actor" or "agent" in someone's journey, but we are often silent about God's saving presence and action in our lives.

In the biblical perspective, God calls us to leave what is familiar and to walk into the unknown. In other words, God initiates our journeys.

Further, God meets us on our way. Indeed, God desires our conversion or personal transformation, after which we relate in new, more beneficial ways to ourselves, other people, and the earth as we proceed toward our life's goal: God and our true selves. In the Old Testament, the drama of God calling people and acting in their lives occurs in the story of the fictional figure Jonah, as well as in the narratives concerning a historical event, namely, the exodus, in which Moses and the Israelites escaped from slavery in Egypt, crossed the Red Sea, and trekked through the Sinai desert to the Holy Land. In the New Testament, God calls Jesus at his baptism, and Jesus affirms his commitment to God during his temptations in the desert (Mark 1:9-13).

The Bible's witness to God's role in human journeys prompts the question, in what ways is God present and active in our lives? Could it be that we have not noticed God's gracious outreach to us or that we have not known how to talk about our religious experiences?

This chapter studies the book of Jonah and part of the book of Exodus. In particular, it illumines these texts' testimonies concerning our potential journeys in response to God's gift of *salus*, salvation. In the biblical perspective, God takes the initiative in creating us and in trying to bring us to personal wholeness beyond death. At the same time, God asks us to discover and accept ourselves as God's treasure and to work with God in realizing our God-given personal identities. In other words, I am like a loose-knit group of potentially talented singers. Their underdeveloped voices represent my untapped talents. With God's guidance and encouragement, I can form these voices into a choir, my whole self. Further, I may join with other persons as they are developing their respective voices into harmonious choirs, and I can imagine the "day" when we shall participate in the choir of God's new creation (Rev 5:13).

According to the Bible, the crucial process in our journeys involves us acknowledging God as God and ourselves as God's pearls of great value (Matt 13:46). This profound act of saying yes to God and to ourselves is called *metanoia* (Greek), meaning a "change of heart and mind." It is also known as personal transformation, as both conversion (Latin *convertere*, "to turn around") and repentance (Latin *re*, "again," and *paenitire*, "to feel sorrow"). As defined in the *Catechism of the Catholic Church*, conversion is "a radical reorientation of our whole life, a return, a conversion to God with all our heart, an end of sin, a turning away from evil, . . . [and] the desire and resolution to change one's life, with hope in God's mercy and trust in the help of grace."[1] In other words, *metanoia* is the turning from one's false self, sin, to God and to one's true self, as envisioned and bestowed by God. It involves nothing less than the decentering of one's ego and one's recentering in God. Needless to say, this transformation does not occur in an instant. A person's *metanoia* is an ongoing process during his or her entire life—a process that manifests itself at specific moments or turning points in one's life.[2]

Let's examine the process of *metanoia* as described in the book of Jonah and also in the book of Exodus, where we will also encounter the biblical belief that God is Yahweh, "the One who causes [us] to be" (Exod 3:14). This inquiry will conclude with a reflection on the paradox of love and freedom in our lives.

I. Personal Transformation in the Book of Jonah

The book of Jonah is a story about the conversion of a fictional figure, Jonah. It was written in the fifth century BC as the people of Israel were rethinking their views of God, themselves, and their non-Jewish neighbors. In the aftermath of their enslavement or exile in Babylon, they were moving toward a more complex understanding of God and also of the human response to the divine gift of *salus*. In this historical context, the book of Jonah accentuates the mystery of God's gift and the nature of personal transformation.

A. The Book's Literary Elements

The book of Jonah recounts two fictional conversions, the one of an Israelite prophet, Jonah, and the other of the non-Jewish people of Nineveh, a city in today's Iraq.

According to the story, God called Jonah to go east to Nineveh and preach repentance to its citizens. Rejecting his divine call and hence his God-given personal identity, Jonah boarded a ship at Joppa headed to Tarshish, a city in present-day Turkey or Spain. In other words, Jonah chose to go west instead of east and thus away "from the presence of the LORD" (Jonah 1:3). When a storm arose on the Mediterranean Sea and threatened the ship, the crew determined that Jonah had brought this misfortune upon them by disobeying a deity. Jonah admitted his guilt and said, "Pick me up and throw me into the sea" (1:12). The sailors tossed Jonah into the tumultuous waters, and the storm abated. Jonah was then swallowed by "a large fish." In the fish's "belly" (or the "Pit" [2:6]), he "prayed to the LORD his God" (2:1). After "three days and three nights," the fish "spewed Jonah out upon the dry land" (2:10). Jonah prayed a psalm of thanksgiving: "I called to the LORD out of my distress, and he answered me; out of the belly of Sheol I cried, and you heard my voice" (2:2). This psalm ends with Jonah's recognition of God's salvific love: "Deliverance belongs to the LORD!" (2:9).

God called Jonah "a second time" (Jonah 3:1), and Jonah accepted his call. Going to Nineveh, he walked through its streets, declaring that God would punish the Ninevites for their sins. Learning of Jonah's message, Nineveh's king decreed that the people should "turn from their evil ways" (3:8). Thus, everyone underwent *metanoia*. Seeing the Ninevites' repentance, God did not allow the people's "calamity" (3:10).

God's forgiveness of the Ninevites had a twofold impact on Jonah. First, it opened Jonah's eyes to the fathomless depths and universal breadth of God's offer of salvation, of *salus*: "You are a gracious God and merciful, slow to anger, and abounding in steadfast love, and ready to relent from punishing" (Jonah 4:2). Second, God's forgiveness of the Ninevites upset Jonah, who "became angry." He prayed, "O LORD, please take my life from me" (4:1, 3). Why? He wanted to be a prophet whose message of doom came true, even if it brought calamity upon the Ninevites. Thus, he was more concerned about his prestige and his power than about the well-being of God's people.

Seeing Jonah's preoccupation with himself, God directed a bush to grow up near Jonah so that its shade would protect the prophet (Jonah 4:6). Indeed, Jonah became comfortable in its shade. Then God sent a worm to kill the bush. When Jonah became upset about the loss of the bush, God posed a rhetorical question to him: If Jonah could grieve over the bush's destruction, should not God's grief be much greater if God's people in Nineveh had not repented? At this, the book ends. It remains unanswered whether Jonah would let go of his egotism and thus advance the *metanoia* he had begun in the "belly of the fish."

B. The Process of Personal Transformation

The book of Jonah sheds light on God's gift of salvation and also on our acceptance of God's *salus*.

The book uses the imagery of God unleashing a storm upon the ship, threatening to send "calamity" upon Nineveh, and directing "a worm" to attack the bush. By means of these images, it communicates that God passionately wants Jonah and the Ninevites to return to God. God does not turn away from God's people but persists in trying to get their attention when they ignore God's love. In particular, God patiently reaches out to Jonah three times: God initially calls Jonah (1:2), then calls Jonah a second time (3:1), and lastly tries to shock Jonah out of his selfishness (4:7). God's love is persistent, fathomless, and universal. As the book attests, God seeks the salvation of Gentiles, such as the Ninevites, as well as of the people of Israel.

What does the book of Jonah teach about *metanoia*? First, Jonah is similar to Adam and Eve in that he initially rejects God's call, God's invitation to growth in personal identity. There's the inclination in Jonah—and in us—to be displeased with the self and the talents that we have received at birth. In this regard, Thomas Merton writes, "In order to become myself I must cease to be what I always thought I wanted to be, and in order to find myself I must go out of myself, and in order to live I have to die."[3] With these words, the Trappist monk alludes to Jesus' call to repentance: "For those who want to save their life will lose it, and those who lose their life for my sake will find it" (Matt 16:25).

Second, the book of Jonah illumines five phases in someone's personal transformation.

Phase 1: A false self. Jonah flees from God and his God-given self (1:3). In short, he opts for radical autonomy.

Phase 2: Loss. Amid the storm, Jonah decides to stop fleeing from God and from his identity. He lets go of his false self as he tells the sailors, "Throw me into the sea" (1:12).

Phase 3: Waiting for God. Jonah finds himself in the "belly of the fish," in the "belly of Sheol," in the "Pit" (1:17; 2:2, 6). At this point, Jonah opts for theonomy; he reorients himself toward God: "Jonah prayed to the LORD from the belly of the fish" (2:1).

Phase 4: Discovery of God's gift. After "three days and three nights," Jonah receives God's gift. Raised by God out of the "Pit," he says, "Deliverance belongs to the LORD" (2:9).

Phase 5: Toward one's true self. In response to God's call, Jonah moves toward his true self, though not without difficulties. That he is angry after God forgives the Ninevites shows the persistence of Jonah's dark urge to be in control. Having undergone his decisive reorientation toward God, he must be transformed further by God's grace. He must live in theonomy.

A person's *metanoia* is a lifelong process in which radical turning points occur. In this regard, the late secretary general of the United Nations Dag Hammarskjold (d. 1961) wrote in his diary, at age fifty-six, that his *metanoia* at an earlier age had shaped his entire life. He tragically died in Africa soon after writing these words: "I don't know Who—or what—put the question, I don't know when it was put. I don't even remember answering. But at some moment I did answer *Yes* to Someone—or Something—and from that hour I was certain that existence is meaningful and that, therefore, my life, in self-surrender, had a goal. Whitsunday, 1961."[4]

The book of Jonah's emphasis in the fifth century BC on conversion or personal transformation was not new in ancient Israel. Over many centuries, the Israelite prophets had repeatedly issued God's call for repentance. In the early sixth century BC, Jeremiah had warned the people of Jerusalem, especially the priests, that they would undergo great suffering if they did not turn back to God. Yet he also assured them that when they returned to God, God would "give them a heart to know that I am the LORD" (Jer 24:7). In the mid-eighth century BC, Hosea had anticipated the day when the Israelites in the northern kingdom amid their hardship would repent, saying, "Come, let us return to the LORD; for it is he who has torn, and he will heal us; he has struck down, and he will bind us up. After two days he will revive us; on the third day he will raise us up, that we may live before him" (Hos 6:1-2). Even earlier, in the tenth century BC, the prophet Nathan had confronted King David concerning his adultery with Bathsheba and concerning his plot against Bathsheba's husband, Uriah. In response, David repented of his wrongdoing and declared, "I have sinned against the LORD" (2 Sam 12:13).

Israel's history of *metanoia* is striking. Yet it is not surprising, for conversion or personal transformation was central in Israel's foundational event, the exodus. This defining moment of liberation involved not only God's offer of deliverance, salvation, to Moses and the Hebrew slaves but also their conversion and yes to God's *salus*. Guided by this metaphor of God's gift and our acceptance of it, let us study biblical testimonies concerning the exodus.

II. The Exodus as Israel's Conversion

In the Old Testament, the primary event of God's salvation is the exodus. It is commemorated every spring by the Jewish people in the feast of Passover. Although the event can be summarized in a few sentences, it generated numerous testimonies among the ancient Israelites.

A. The Bare Facts

In about 1250 BC, a large number of Hebrew slaves, Israelites, escaped from their work camps in Egypt, which was ruled at the time by Pharaoh Ramses II. Their exodus or departure was likely made possible by natural disasters or "plagues" that weakened Ramses II's control of the people. Led by Moses, the Israelites fled eastward into the Egyptian desert. They were pursued by the pharaoh's soldiers. At the Red Sea—or, more accurately, at the Sea of Reeds—they made their way through the marsh. However, the Egyptian soldiers with their horses and chariots became bogged down in the mud and stopped their pursuit of the runaway slaves. Reaching dry ground, Moses and the Israelites fled into the Sinai desert. At some point, they adopted the Ten Commandments as the cornerstone of their "covenant" or agreement with God. Afterward, they settled in "a land flowing with milk and honey" (Exod 3:17).

There's no doubt that the exodus occurred. Nor is there any doubt that this liberation has had lasting significance for the Jewish people and hence also for Christians.

B. The Sources, Contexts, and Literary Accounts

Differing accounts of the exodus emerged in Israel's oral traditions, some of which date back to the event itself. Subsequently, at various times, scribes wrote down these oral traditions, simultaneously enriching them with their own insights into the exodus. Further, they eventually united these literary units into texts, or they inserted these units into already existing texts.

We'll start with the most ancient of these biblical texts. Soon after their escape in 1250 BC, the former slaves recounted the event in a folk song, which is now Exodus 15:1-21. The song begins and ends with the refrain "Sing to the LORD, for he has triumphed gloriously; horse and rider he has thrown into the sea" (Exod 15:1, 21). The song recounts in imaginative language what occurred: "Pharaoh's chariots and his army [God] cast into the sea; [Pharaoh's] picked officers were sunk in the Red Sea. The floods covered them; they went down into the depths like a stone" (15:4-5). This song circulated orally for three centuries until it was written down.

In the mid-900s BC, J (the Jahwist source) wrote a succinct narrative of the exodus, which—similar to the ancient folk song—was meant not to impart detailed information but to witness to God's salvific act on behalf of the slaves. J's narrative is now the core text of Exodus 14. In fashioning this account, J was guided by at least three theological convictions: God is immanent in human events; God can act in natural occurrences; and God makes unilateral covenants that invite our faith in God. Thus, according to J, the Israelites escaped because of a series of seemingly "coincidental" natural occurrences. As the slaves fled eastward, a fog or "the pillar of cloud" rolled in; it separated the slaves from the Egyptian soldiers (Exod 14:19). Then night fell, and there arose "a strong east wind all night" that "turned the sea into dry land; and the waters were divided" (14:21). The runaway slaves advanced "on dry ground," and the soldiers "pursued" them. Just before dawn, a thunderstorm— "the pillar of fire and cloud"—swept in "and threw the Egyptian army into a panic," as lightning terrified them and their animals (14:24). At dawn, the east wind ceased. "The waters returned and covered the chariots and chariot drivers" (14:28). The soldiers perished, but the Israelites "walked on dry ground through the sea" (14:29).

J's account of the exodus was not fully satisfactory to E (the Elohist source), who worked in northern Israel in about 850 BC. According to E, God is wholly transcendent and thus intervenes in human affairs by sending angels among us. Further, E was keenly aware of sin, of our tendency to turn away from God. Influenced by these theological convictions and perhaps also by ancient oral traditions, E inserted some additional verses into J's narrative. E added that as the Israelites neared the Sea of Reeds, they feared that they would be trapped between the soldiers and the water. Their lack of faith in God resulted in their complaining to Moses, "Was it because there were no graves in Egypt that you have taken us away to die in the wilderness?" (Exod 14:11). According to E, the Israelites succeeded because "the angel of God" initially led them and then "went behind them" in the fog in order to delay the Egyptians (14:19).

The narrative of J and E was edited again in about 450 BC when P (the Priestly source) inserted verses into the account. These additions express P's theological conviction that we must engage in religious rituals in order to respond appropriately to God's offer of salvation. Also, P held that God's interventions in our lives are somewhat obvious miracles. Thus, according to P, God required that Moses hold up his staff and "stretch out his hand over the sea" (Exod 14:16). After Moses performed this ritual, God "drove the sea back" (14:21). The Israelites went ahead amid a miracle, "the waters forming a wall for them on their right and on their left" (14:22, 29). Thus, "the waters were divided" (14:21), similar to how they had been "gathered together into one place" by God at the dawn of creation (Gen 1:9). Further, after the Israelites were on dry ground, God again instructed Moses: "Stretch out your hand over the sea, so that the water may come back upon the Egyptians, upon their chariots and the chariot drivers" (Exod 14:26). When Moses did this ritual, "the sea returned to its normal depth," thus drowning the Egyptians (14:27).

In sum, Exodus 14 was originally written by J and subsequently edited by E and then later by P. Evolving over five hundred years, it now precedes in the Bible the more ancient folk song in Exodus 15. However, Exodus 14 and Exodus 15 do not exhaust the Old Testament's accounts of the exodus.

Working in Jerusalem in 620 BC, D (the Deuteronomic source) likely edited and wrote down an oral tradition concerning the exodus. This story, now in Deuteronomy 26:5-9, tells of the patriarch Jacob, the "wandering Aramean," who led the Israelites into Egypt, where the Israelites increased in number and "became a great nation" (Deut 26:5). But the Egyptians eventually "treated us harshly and afflicted us, by imposing hard labor on us" (26:6). In slavery "we cried to the Lord," and "the Lord heard our voice and saw our affliction, our toil, and our oppression. The Lord brought us out of Egypt with a mighty hand and an outstretched arm, with a terrifying display of power, and with signs and wonders; and he brought us into this place and gave us this land, a land flowing with milk and honey" (26:7-9).

According to D, the believing community's remembrance of God's deliverance of Moses and the Israelites should occur whenever Israelites make their annual pilgrimage to Jerusalem's temple. At the temple, the pilgrims should recount God's gift of salvation in the exodus and then gratefully acknowledge God's *salus* in their rituals. To make this point, D placed the oral tradition concerning the exodus (Deut 26:5-9) within D's description of the pilgrims bringing fruit and vegetables to

Jerusalem's temple, handing them to the priests for sacrifices of praise, and then giving thanks to God: "So now I bring the first of the fruit of the ground that you, O LORD, have given me" (26:10).

Testimony concerning the exodus also occurs in the psalms, the songs that the Israelites composed between 1000 BC and 200 BC. Psalm 66:6, for example, declares that God "turned the sea into dry land; they passed through the river on foot. There we rejoiced in him." Psalm 77:19-20 proclaims, "Your way was through the sea, your path, through the mighty waters; yet your footsteps were unseen. You led your people like a flock by the hand of Moses and Aaron." Psalm 114:1-3 states, "When Israel went out from Egypt, the house of Jacob from a people of a strange language, Judah became God's sanctuary, Israel his dominion. The sea looked and fled; Jordan turned back."

Finally, the prophet Second Isaiah viewed the return of the Israelites to Jerusalem in 538 BC, after their Babylonian exile, as their new exodus. Writing shortly before their liberation by King Cyrus of Persia, the prophet wrote: "Thus says the LORD, who makes a way in the sea, a path in the mighty waters, who brings out chariot and horse, army and warrior; . . . Do not remember the former things, or consider the things of old. I am about to do a new thing; . . . I will make a way in the wilderness and rivers in the desert" (Isa 43:16-19).

These texts—Exodus 15, Exodus 14, Deuteronomy 26:6-9, Psalm 66, Psalm 77, Psalm 114, and Isaiah 43—give differing accounts of the same event. Why? Why are there so many testimonies? The exodus is the definitive event of God's deliverance or salvation of the Israelites and of Israel's yes, its conversion, in response to God's gift. As such, the exodus is always to be remembered by God's people, who in remembering the exodus will relive Israel's reception and acceptance of God's *salus*. As the community remembers and celebrates God's gift and the Israelites' yes at the Sea of Reeds in 1250 BC, it shares anew in the exodus, renews its *metanoia*, and lives with fresh gratitude to God and with greater readiness to serve God's people. For this reason, Jewish people commemorate the exodus every spring in their Seder during Passover (see Exod 12:1-18).

C. The Process of Personal Transformation

Although the numerous biblical accounts of the exodus differ in their specific imagery, they agree that this one event decisively reveals that

God is our salvation (Ps 27:1) and that in response to the divine gift of *salus* we should undergo *metanoia*. These diverse texts work together to convey the five phases of conversion that we saw in the book of Jonah.

Phase 1: A false self, slavery. The Hebrew slaves in Egypt found themselves in harsh circumstances. They were required to live in heteronomy, that is, in strict adherence to the pharaoh and their slave masters. As a young man, Moses "saw their forced labor. He saw an Egyptian beating a Hebrew, one of his kinsfolk." Outraged by this injustice, Moses "killed the Egyptian and hid him in the sand" (Exod 2:11-12). Moses also saw that, as a result of their oppressive situation, the Israelites directed their anger about their slavery at one another. When he came upon one slave abusing another, he asked him, "Why do you strike your fellow Hebrew?" (2:13).

Although the Israelites wanted their freedom, they were reluctant to take the risk to obtain it. Such is the case in all forms of heteronomy. The Israelites' inclination to stay with what was familiar and relatively secure also showed itself during their exodus. When they thought that they might perish at the Sea of Reeds, they complained to Moses that it would have been "better for us to serve the Egyptians than to die in the wilderness" (Exod 14:12). Later, after entering the Sinai desert and going without food and water, they yearned to return to their slave quarters in Egypt. They said to Moses, "If only we had died by the hand of the Lord in the land of Egypt, when we sat by the fleshpots and ate our fill of bread" (16:3). These statements evince our human tendency to keep the status quo, to stay in our current form of life, no matter how much it blocks us from moving toward God and from becoming whole persons.

Phase 2: Loss, disruption. The state of affairs in Egypt was destabilized by natural disasters, the plagues: the pollution of the Nile River, frogs, gnats, flies, a cattle blight, boils, hail and rain, locusts, the "darkness" caused by the sand in the desert wind (called the *khamsin*), and finally the death of the Egyptian children (Exod 7:8–11:10). These catastrophes are attributed to God by some of the biblical writers. But is this an appropriate claim? Does God afflict people? (See chap. 4.) In any case, these natural disasters disrupted the normal routines of the Egyptians and their Hebrew slaves; they coalesced to form an opportunity for the escape of Moses and the Israelites.

Moses had emerged as the slaves' leader. He had returned to Egypt after receiving God's call at Mount Horeb, which is also called Mount

Sinai, where he was tending sheep (Exod 3:10; 6:2-9). In this divine encounter, Moses learned God's name: Yahweh, "the One who causes [us] to be" (see chap. 1; also see below). In this religious experience, Moses was stripped of his identity as a shepherd and received God's call to his new identity as the Israelites' leader. In response, Moses began to prepare the Hebrew slaves for their escape (4:18–6:30).

Amid the disruption that the plagues caused in Egyptian society, Moses seized the opportunity and initiated the exodus. The Israelites departed from their slave quarters, fleeing eastward (Exod 12:37-39). They "went up out of the land of Egypt prepared for battle" (13:18). But their elation was soon deflated. They panicked when they felt trapped between the Egyptian solders and the Sea of Reeds. "In great fear the Israelites cried out to the LORD" (14:10).

Phase 3: Waiting for God. Aware that runaway slaves could not rely on their own strength and cunning, Moses urged them to trust God, to fall into the unknown: "Do not be afraid, stand firm, and see the deliverance that the LORD will accomplish for you today. . . . The LORD will fight for you, and you have only to keep still" (Exod 14:13-14). In other words, Moses directed the Israelites to wait for God to enlighten and to empower them through the apparent impasse. Doing what Moses said, the Israelites entrusted their lives to God, to the "higher power." In this surrender, they allowed the decentering of their egos and their recentering in the LORD, life's Source and Goal.

Phase 4: Discovery of God's gift. The Israelites saw that a desert fog had unexpectedly rolled in, blocking them from the view of the soldiers who were pursuing them. "The pillar of cloud . . . took its place behind them. It came between the army of Egypt and the army of Israel." Then the sun went down, and "one [group] did not come near the other all night." But "the LORD drove the sea back by a strong east wind all night, and turned the sea into dry land." Seeing the exposed sandbars, the Israelites immediately advanced "on dry ground" (Exod 14:19-22).

"The Egyptians pursued, and went into the sea after them, all of Pharaoh's horses, chariots, and chariot drivers. At the morning watch the LORD in the pillar of fire and cloud looked down upon the Egyptian army, and threw the Egyptian army into panic. He clogged their chariot wheels so that they turned with difficulty. The Egyptians said, 'Let us flee from the Israelites.'" The east wind suddenly subsided, "and at dawn the sea returned to its normal depth. . . . The waters returned and covered the chariots and the chariot drivers, the entire army of Pharaoh . . . ; not one of them remained. But the Israelites walked on dry ground through the sea. . . . Israel saw the Egyptians dead on the seashore. . . . The people feared the LORD and believed in the LORD and in his servant Moses" (Exod 14:23-31).

At this point, the Israelites praised and thanked God. "Then Moses and the Israelites sang this song to the LORD: 'I will sing to the LORD, for he has triumphed gloriously; horse and rider he has thrown into the sea. The LORD is my strength and my might, and he has become my salvation'" (Exod 15:1-2). In thanking God, they acknowledged that the LORD is their salvation, the one who liberated them from slavery. They sang, "Your right hand, O LORD, shattered the enemy" (15:6). Also, "the prophet Miriam, Aaron's sister, took a tambourine in her hand; and all the women went out after her with tambourines and with dancing." Miriam sang, "Sing to the LORD, for he has triumphed gloriously; horse and rider he has thrown into the sea" (15:20-21).

Phase 5: Accepting one's true self. God's saving presence and action for the Israelites at the Sea of Reeds did not eliminate the Israelites' free will. God did not demand that they relinquish their personal freedom. On the contrary, as the Israelites surrendered their egos and were recentered in God, they experienced even greater freedom to shape their destiny as they made their way through the Sinai desert. However, while they had drawn closer to God in their conversion at the Sea of Reeds, they soon wavered in their faith in God. They doubted God's saving love for them when they could not drink the water of Marah (Exod 15:22-25), had no bread to eat (16:2-3), and became thirsty at Massah (17:1-7). It was important, therefore, that the Israelites adopt a new form of life, theonomy, so that they could sustain their *metanoia.*

At Mount Sinai, God invited Moses and the Israelites to enter into a new covenant or pledge concerning a form of life or "law" that would give them the freedom to respond appropriately to God's gift of *salus.* God said to them: "You have seen what I did to the Egyptians, and how I bore you on eagles' wings and brought you to myself. Now, therefore, if you obey my voice and keep my covenant, you shall be my treasured possession out of all the peoples. Indeed, the whole earth is mine" (Exod 19:4-6). In order to maintain and nurture the freedom that came with the exodus, God gave the people the Ten Commandments (Exod 20:1-17; Deut 5:6-21), which the Israelites promised to obey (Exod 24:1-11; Josh 24:1-28).

The Ten Commandments, also called the Decalogue, direct their adherents to freedom. That is, they define a form of life in which people do not abuse one another, as occurred in Egypt when one slave would strike another (Exod 2:13). This new orientation toward God also entails mutual respect and care for one another, as took place when the people traversed the Sea of Reeds and when they subsequently sang together (15:20-21). To put this another way, the Ten Commandments direct us away from radical heteronomy, from enslavement to other human beings or to objects of desire (4:27-31), and they also direct us away from radical autonomy, from self-idolatry in our golden calves (32:1-4). To put it positively, the Ten Commandments demand our theonomy as they steer us toward the true God and our true selves. As the book of Sirach 15:1-3 states, "Whoever holds to the law will obtain wisdom. She will come to meet him like a mother, and like a young bride she will welcome him. She will feed him with the bread of learning, and give him the water of wisdom to drink."

In conclusion, what does the exodus as remembered in the biblical testimonies reveal about God and about us? It discloses God's gracious offer of deliverance or liberation to us and our appropriate response of affirmation and gratitude. In light of this beneficial dynamism in our lives, let us reflect on the belief that God is the Lord, Yahweh. This inquiry will bring us to the paradox that as we surrender ourselves to God, we gain the freedom to become individuated persons in relation to God.

III. God: Life's Source and Goal

When a parent works two jobs in order to pay the bills, she shows her love for her family through her action. When a teacher voluntarily tutors struggling students after school, he discloses through his time and energy his commitment to the education of young people. In sum, someone's actions often disclose the person's deepest values and personal character.

Now extend this line of thought to God's "act" of delivering the Israelites from slavery and leading them to freedom in the land of milk and honey. God's "work" in the exodus reveals God's love for the well-being of God's people; it demonstrates God's abiding desire to give us the fullness of life, (*salus*.) In short, this divine action discloses God's deepest values and personal character.

According to the J, E, and P sources, God has even explained what God's action in the exodus reveals about God. Wanting to leave no ambiguity about God's intention in saving the enslaved Israelites, God spoke to Moses prior to the exodus. In the burning bush, God not only called Moses to lead the people to freedom but also revealed to him God's intention and its wellspring in God's very being.

Exodus 3:1-15 (written by both J and E) recounts that when Moses was tending sheep near Mount Horeb (Mount Sinai), he came upon a bush that "was blazing, yet it was not consumed" (Exod 3:2). As he walked toward it, "God called to him out of the bush, 'Moses! Moses!'" Disposing himself to the unknown, to mystery, Moses answered, "Here I am." God said, "I am the God of your father, the God of Abraham, the God of Isaac, and the God of Jacob" (3:6). Having identified himself, God then added, "I have observed the misery of my people. . . . I have come down to deliver them from the Egyptians, and to bring them up out of that land to a good and broad land, a land flowing with milk and honey" (3:7-8). With these words, God clarified the divine intention at work in the exodus. Then God charged Moses to assist in bringing God's gift of *salus* to the Israelites: "So come, I will send you to Pharaoh to bring my people, the Israelites, out of Egypt" (3:10).

Moses immediately asked God whether he, Moses, was the right person for this task: "Who am I that I should go to Pharaoh, and bring the Israelites out of Egypt?" Having seen himself as a shepherd, Moses was asking about his personal identity. God answered, "I will be with you" (Exod 3:11-12). What assuring words! They mean that Moses would be responding to God's call and realizing his true identity as he accepted God's call. God was offering Moses salvation, *salus*, and God was awaiting Moses' grateful yes.

Being cautious, Moses wondered whether God could be trusted. Would God stick with Moses through thick and thin? Was God acting on a divine whim, or was God's intention anchored in God's being, in God's identity? Seeking an answer, Moses asked to learn God's "name" (Exod 3:13). In the ancient world, to know someone's name was to have an intimate bond with this person. It was to know the person's soul, and hence it brought the potential to have power over the person, who was now vulnerable. Nevertheless, God told Moses the divine name in three forms: "I AM WHO I AM," "I AM," and "Yahweh" or, more accurately, "YHWH" since vowels did not then exist in Hebrew.

God adds that this name—in its three forms—identifies "the God of your ancestors, the God of Abraham, of Isaac, and of Jacob" (3:14-15).

In order to grasp the significance of God's name, let's consider three aspects of Exodus 3:14-15. First, the ancient Israelites developed such reverence and gratitude for God's name that they chose not to speak the divine name but to use in its place the title "LORD," *Adonai* in Hebrew. "LORD" appears today in most English-language Bibles in place of "Yahweh." The sacred character of God's name is conveyed in Exodus 6:2-3, which was written by P and amplifies Exodus 3:14-15: "God also spoke to Moses and said to him: 'I am the LORD. I appeared to Abraham, Isaac, and Jacob as God Almighty [*El Shaddai*], but by my name 'The LORD' [YHWH] I did not make myself known to them.'" God has entrusted to God's people the divine name, which we would not have otherwise known.

Second, the divine name's three forms—"I AM WHO I AM," "I AM," and "Yahweh"—are etymologically rooted in the verb "to be," *hayah* in Hebrew. The divine name means, therefore, that God is "to be," "the One who causes [us] to be" (Exod 3:14-15). In other words, God is the One who truly lives and gives life to everything else that is. God is life's Source and Goal, the Alpha and the Omega, the Beginning and the End of our lives and creation (Rev 1:8).

Third, the divine name is not a name in the ordinary sense. It designates the One who cannot be named because God is not one object or entity among others. Rather, God is the ultimate mystery; God is the indefinable, inexhaustible, transcendent yet immanent reality who is absolutely gracious. Indeed, God lovingly creates us with the intention of giving us *salus*, that is, well-being, the fullness of life. This aspect of God's name comes to expression in Exodus 33; as Moses and the Israelites were trekking through the Sinai desert, God told them a fourth form of the divine name: "I will be gracious to whom I will be gracious, and will show mercy on whom I will show mercy" (Exod 33:19). In other words, God's name is this: "I will love you because I am love, not because you earned my love." God is selfless love, agape (cf. 1 John 4:16-19).

Let's return to the idea that God's action in the exodus disclosed God's intention to give the enslaved Israelites the fullness of life. We can now add that the exodus revealed not only God's intention but also God's personal identity as YHWH, as "the One who causes [us] to be." God's delivering the people from slavery and leading them to *begin.* *end.*

freedom confirmed that God is Yahweh. What God did for the ancient Israelites at the Sea of Reeds has disclosed who God is: <u>life's Source and Goal</u>, <u>the Alpha and the Omega</u>, who is committed to creating us and granting us the fullness of life.

Interestingly, the Lord Jesus knew and confirmed the divine name, Yahweh. For example, he upheld God's name with its saving significance when he was confronted by some Sadducees. After these Jewish priests ridiculed belief in God's general resurrection of the dead, Jesus asserted that they had failed to understand God's name as disclosed to Moses at Mount Horeb: "And as for the dead being raised, have you not read in the book of Moses [Exod 3:14-15], in the story about the bush, how God said to him, 'I am the God of Abraham, the God of Isaac, and the God of Jacob'? He is God not of the dead, but of the living; you are quite wrong" (Mark 12:26-27). Jesus left no doubt that Abba is YHWH, "the One who causes [us] to be"—to be even beyond death! God, Abba, is the Source and Goal of our lives now and in eternity.

In the Old Testament, God's salvation of the Israelites was God's single most important revelatory and salvific action on behalf of the Israelites. It disclosed that God is the "deliverer" (Ps 18:2), "salvation" (Pss 27:1; 62:1), and "the Savior" (Isa 45:15). Because God is life's Source and Goal, God calls us to move beyond slavery and death to freedom and life. What God asks of us is what God asked of Moses and the Hebrew slaves: *metanoia*, conversion, the decentering of our egos and our recentering in the LORD, in "the One who causes [us] to be."

IV. The Paradox of Love and Freedom

A few years ago, two birds built a nest on top of a light fixture on our garage—a lamp that we could clearly see from a kitchen window. One day, we noticed that there were three eggs in the nest and that the birds were taking turns sitting on the eggs. After the eggs hatched, the three chicks were constantly receiving food from their parents. Then one morning the birds were screeching more than usual. The parents were perched in a nearby tree, and the three chicks were standing on the edge of the nest flapping their wings. By noon, two of the chicks had flown from the nest, but the third chick was still in the nest. It would stand on the nest's edge, begin to flap its wings, and then back away from the edge. Meanwhile, the parents were screeching at it from the bushes. Occasionally, one of the parents would fly to the nest and fuss with the frightened little one. Just before sundown, the third chick took to flight. After that, the nest remained empty.

This drama of the birds points to a paradoxical truth: the love we receive nurtures our freedom in relation to the one who loves us. Love sets "the other" free to become "the other." In the case of birds, this dynamism is simple: the parents nurture their chicks, and the chicks fly off to lead independent lives. With us, however, things are much more complex.

We show that our parents have loved us when we leave them, when we become financially, emotionally, and intellectually independent in relation to our parents. As we earn a salary, pay our utility bills, and establish our circles of friends, we increasingly stand apart from our parents. Yet as we gain independence and individuation, we are able to relate in new, more mature ways to our parents and grow even closer to them. Here's a paradox of personal development and hence also of God's grace in our lives: the greater the authentic love among persons, the greater the freedom in their personal relationships. Conversely, as the true freedom among persons gets greater, the greater is the love in their personal relationships.

In contrast, lack of love between parents and children results in a lack of independence and hence of individuation. Adults who were neglected or abused in their childhoods usually have difficulty differentiating themselves from their parents. Even though they may become financially independent, they will likely possess inappropriate dependence on or emotional entanglements with their parents unless they receive counseling and establish healthy interpersonal ties with other people, with an alternative "family." Tragically, abuse often binds the abused to their abusers. Yet when there is authentic love, then trust and forgiveness empower people to become independent and differentiated in relation to those who love them.

In chapter 2, we considered the twofold truth that love presupposes freedom and that freedom can nurture love. Reflecting on the tale "Beauty and the Beast," we noted that because the Beast cannot compel Belle to love him, he must allow her to leave the castle and to return only if she wishes. Love presupposes freedom. Conversely, freedom can nurture love. Outside the castle, Belle becomes aware of her love for the Beast and chooses to go back to him.

Now, a third aspect of love and freedom has come before us. Authentic love frees its recipient for greater personal wholeness and hence for increasing personal differentiation in relation to the one who has bestowed the love. At the same time, as someone becomes more individuated, more of an "I," he or she is more capable of becoming a "we," a more mature person growing in true communion with other mature, centered persons. In this vein, the poet Rainer Maria Rilke writes that authentic love "consists of two solitudes which protect, border, and greet each other."[5]

What about the relationship between God and us? God does not intend for us to become divine replicas. Rather, God desires each of us to become "the other," an individuated human person who is God's intimate dialogue partner. As God draws us into greater union with God, God simultaneously enables us to realize our distinct God-given personal identities. In order for this relationship to unfold, God invites us to entrust ourselves to God so that, becoming more united with God, we simultaneously move toward our personal wholeness in differentiation from God. This dynamism of love and freedom is also known as the movement of grace and independence, of personal union and personal differentiation.

Isn't the paradox of grace and independence clear in Moses, Deborah, Samuel, Elijah, and Jeremiah? Isn't it evident too in Jesus, Peter, and Mary of Magdalena? Finally, isn't the dynamism of union and differentiation at work too in holy women and holy men such as St. Francis of Assisi, St. Teresa of Ávila, and Mother Teresa of Calcutta? As each of these holy people placed greater trust in God and found his or her center in God, each became a vibrant, creative, and self-giving person in dialogue with God, even in their questioning God and arguing with God. Theonomy did not stifle them; rather, it generated their individuation and their new experiences of God's presence and even God's absence.

Left to ourselves, we could never imagine that our relationship with God involves the paradox of love and freedom. Yet healthy experiences of interpersonal love among us can teach us otherwise and prompt us to trust in God. We can learn that when we choose lives of radical heteronomy or radical autonomy, we find ourselves enslaved to "false gods"—for example, to manipulative "friends" or to our own controlling egos. But when we undergo a *metanoia* in response to God's grace, we live in theonomy toward God and also toward personal wholeness.

In the Old Testament, the exodus is God's most decisive act of self-revelation and salvation in the history of ancient Israel. As such, it demonstrates God's gift of *salus* to God's people and also the appropriate human response, namely, conversion. As we'll study in chapters 6, 7, and 8, the New Testament presents the life, death, and resurrection of Jesus Christ as God's decisive act of self-revelation and salvation for all people. Jesus Christ is God's gift of *salus* and also makes possible our total acceptance of salvation. While the exodus brought the Israelites to the Holy Land, it left ambiguity concerning life after death. Yet through his life, death, and resurrection, Jesus Christ has revealed and made possible our ultimate destiny: eternal life in union with the LORD, life's Source and Goal, the Alpha and the Omega (Rev 1:8; 18).

Most of us can identify with Dorothy in *The Wizard of Oz*. Rightly so! This story tells the tale of our possible development from being an insecure child to becoming a self-confident adult who is a subject, an interpersonal being, and a self-agent. However, *The Wizard of Oz* leaves unsaid what becomes clear in the Old Testament and the New Testament: our lives can be adventures that end not in death but in eternal life. Our journeys of faith unfold as we discover and accept our God-given selves in response to God's love. But what are we to make of the misery that can obstruct our way to God? Further, what does the Old Testament mean by the resurrection of the dead? These two topics are the subjects of chapter 4 and chapter 5.

Chapter 4

Suffering
Threats to God's Gift

During the summer of 1968, the Catholic theologian Romano Guardini was gravely ill in Munich. At the age of eighty-three, he knew that his health was waning, and he looked for occasions to visit with his family and friends. In these conversations, he discussed his life, death, and hope. In particular, he anticipated arriving before God, who would likely question him about his life. But Guardini also expected that God would invite his questions. If so, Guardini intended to ask God about human suffering—for example, the suffering he had witnessed in Europe during the two world wars, the Nazi tyranny, and the Holocaust. He "firmly hoped that the angel would not deny him the true answer to the question which no book, not even the Bible, no dogma and no teaching authority, no 'theodicy' or theology, not even his own theology, had been able to answer for him: why, God, these fearful detours on the way to salvation, [why] the suffering of the innocent, why sin?"[1] After months of illness, Romano Guardini died on October 1, 1968.

During his last conversations, Guardini voiced a question that troubles many of us: Why is there human suffering, especially of innocent victims? Or to restate it in the words of Rabbi Harold Kushner, "Why do bad things happen to good people?" This question is so pervasive that it has generated various forms of theodicy (Greek *theos*, "God," and *dike*, "justice"). That is, it has prompted many diverse attempts to justify how God, who is all-good, all-knowing, and all-powerful, seemingly remains silent and ineffective amid human hardship.

As Guardini said, the question of God's relationship to human persons during their suffering has yet to receive a completely satisfactory

61

answer, something that cannot be found even in the Bible. In fact, the question itself is cast in differing forms in the Old Testament. For some biblical writers the question is, why does God send hardship into our lives? Others ask, why does God allow it? And still other writers inquire, how should we live with human suffering? The biblical responses to these three questions are profound and worthy of our consideration.

A definition of "suffering" is necessary at the outset. According to the psychologist-ethicist Sidney Callahan, "Suffering consists of an aversive experience involving severe distress—mine, yours, theirs, or ours."[2] In other words, to suffer is to undergo a perceived threat to or an actual attack on one's well-being. It is to experience apparent opposition to our becoming the "I," the "we," and the "doer" whom God envisions. Using our previous metaphors, we can say that human hardship arises as we are frustrated in our efforts to cooperate with God in discovering and realizing ourselves as God's treasure in the field. Or to put it another way, we suffer when we face apparent resistance to our efforts to develop into the harmonious choirs that God desires us to become. At this point, let us turn to the Bible, which, as Pope John Paul II observed, is "a great book about suffering" (*Salvifici Doloris* 6).

I. The Fall of Jerusalem and the Babylonian Exile

The various biblical views of human suffering emerged as the people of Israel coped with specific tragedies, the foremost of which occurred during the sixth century BC. In 722 BC the northern kingdom, Israel, fell to the Assyrians, while the southern kingdom, Judah, managed to keep its independence. However, in 597 BC Babylon's King Nebuchadnezzar II seized control of Judah and looted Jerusalem's temple and royal palace. During this turmoil, Judah's King Jehoiakim died, after which his son King Jehoiachin and some Judeans were deported to Babylon (Jer 22:13-19). In this vacuum King Zedekiah assumed the throne in Jerusalem, and in 586 BC he led a revolt against King Nebuchadnezzar. Not only did this effort fail, but it also prompted Nebuchadnezzar to have his solders overrun Jerusalem and destroy Jerusalem's temple, built by Solomon in 950 BC. Moreover, Nebuchadnezzar deported to Babylon King Zedekiah, his royal court, and artisans. This Babylonian captivity ended in 538 BC when King Cyrus of Persia—after conquering Babylon—allowed the Israelites to return to Jerusalem.

The tragedy in Judah and Jerusalem during the sixth century BC brought into sharp focus for the Israelites the issue of God's relationship to human suffering. It became a major point of reference for most biblical forms of theodicy. We'll consider some of these forms under three categories: God sends human misery, God allows our suffering, and God seeks to guide our response to suffering.

II. God Sends Suffering

According to some biblical writers, God is the primary agent of our hardships. Although God loves us, God also chooses at times to punish us. In this view, God willed that King Nebuchadnezzar II would conquer Judah and Jerusalem. Why? Consider three answers.

A. *Suffering as God's Wake-Up Call*

According to the Old Testament, God is intent on remaining in a loving relationship with us. God has pledged God's very self to the chosen people in the covenants with Abraham and Sarah (Gen 15), Moses and the Israelites (Exod 20; 24), and King David (2 Sam 7). God desires that these pledges of mutual respect and affection enable us to mature to the point at which we relate to God with our whole selves. Giving voice to this divine yearning, the prophet Jeremiah declared, "The days are surely coming, says the LORD, when I will make a new covenant with the house of Israel and the house of Judah. . . . I will put my law within them, and I will write it on their hearts; and I will be their God, and they shall be my people. . . . They shall all know me, from the least of them to the greatest, says the LORD; for I will forgive their iniquity, and remember their sin no more" (Jer 31:31-34).

But if God loves us so much, then why does God afflict us? According to some biblical writers, God punishes us when we are not faithful to God's covenant, when we turn our backs to God and refuse to have a contrite heart. This view of human suffering was repeatedly conveyed by the biblical prophets (Greek, *pro*, "for," and *phetes*, "speaker") who spoke for God. Although the word "prophecy" usually functions today to mean "prediction," it originally meant "God's word," that is, a divinely inspired, insightful analysis of people's current behavior and its effects on them if they do not change their ways.

The prophet Zephaniah, who preached in Judah during the late 600s, endorsed the religious renewal undertaken by King Josiah

(640–609 BC). He did so because he was alarmed that the Israelites had become more concerned about their economic success and international prominence than about their covenant with God. He warned that if the people did not join in Josiah's renewal and undergo a conversion, they would be subject to God's "wrath," to "the day of the LORD" (Zeph 1:7). He proclaimed, "The great day of the LORD is near. . . . That day will be a day of wrath, a day of distress and anguish" (1:14-15). Impelled by love for Israel, God would inflict his "fierce anger" on sinners and simultaneously spare the people who had returned to God. Zephaniah urged the people, "Seek righteousness, seek humility; perhaps you may be hidden on the day of the LORD's wrath" (2:3). If Zephaniah had lived to see the Babylonians' destruction of Jerusalem's temple, he would have attributed this tragedy to God's wrath.

The prophet Jeremiah took up Zephaniah's call for the Israelites' renewal. As a young man, Jeremiah judged that God had called him at conception to be a prophet. Indeed, God had said, "Before I formed you in the womb I knew you, and before you were born I consecrated you; I appointed you a prophet to the nations" (Jer 1:5). In particular, God intended for him to speak mournful complaints, "jeremiads," against the people of Judah, especially against Jerusalem's priests, kings, and false prophets. According to Jeremiah, although the Israelites were following the externals of their religious belief, they were not truly committed to the LORD. Speaking for God, Jeremiah asserted that the priests were no longer seeking to do God's will; they "did not ask, 'Where is the LORD?'" (2:6). They were too preoccupied with their ceremonies. Moreover, the Israelites' civic leaders had lost their ties to God; thus God observed, "Those who handled the law did not know me." Also, many of Judah's so-called prophets, in fact, "prophesied by Baal [a false god], and went after things that do not profit." Thus Jeremiah spoke for God: "Therefore once more I accuse you, says the LORD, and I accuse your children's children" (2:8-9). According to Jeremiah, God could no longer restrain the divine anger: "I am full of the wrath of the LORD; I am weary of holding it in. Pour it out on the children in the street and on the gatherings of young men as well; both husband and wife shall be taken, the old folk and the very aged" (6:11).

After King Nebuchadnezzar II looted Jerusalem in 597 BC, Jeremiah urged the Israelites to endure their hardships, regarding them as their due punishment for having turned away from God. He also urged King Zedekiah not to revolt against Nebuchadnezzar but to trust that God would save the Israelites after they had completed their time of repentance. But the prophet's words fell on deaf ears: Zedekiah initiated an unsuccessful revolt in 586 BC. Nebuchadnezzar destroyed Jerusalem's temple and deported more Israelites to Babylon (see Jer 29:1-23).

Amid Jerusalem's ruins, Jeremiah proclaimed words of hope. Claiming to speak for God, he said, "I myself will gather the remnant of my flock out of all the lands where I have driven them, and I will bring them back to their fold, and they shall be fruitful and multiply" (Jer 23:3). God spoke as a lover to the beloved: "I have loved you with an everlasting love; therefore I have continued my faithfulness to you. Again I will build you, and you shall be built, O virgin Israel!" (31:3-4). God spoke, too, of renewing the covenant: "I will make a new covenant with the house of Israel and the house of Judah. . . . I will put my law within them, and I will write it on their hearts; and I will be their God, and they shall be my people" (31:31, 33).

B. Suffering as God's Retribution

The Deuteronomic writers, or Deuteronomists, who worked before, during, and after the Babylonian exile (586–538 BC), explained that God punishes us when we fail to follow God's laws, foremost of which are the Ten Commandments. In the books of Deuteronomy, Numbers, and Leviticus, the Deuteronomists (Greek *deuteron*, "second," and *nomos*, "law") compiled the 613 laws that they attributed to Moses.

The Deuteronomists held that God had brought about the conquest of Israel in 722 BC, of Judah in 597 BC, and of Jerusalem in 586 BC. Why had God done these things? God did so in order to discipline the Israelites as a judge might sentence a lawbreaker. Similar to the prophets, the Deuteronomists held that God sends evil into our lives so that we might repent. But they differed from Zephaniah and Jeremiah in that they spoke in legal terms, while the prophets used the interpersonal metaphor of a lover and the beloved.

The Deuteronomists developed their legal metaphor to the point that they highlighted what they perceived to be a recurring legal process in history. The cycle, they said, consists of four phases or steps. Step 1: the people's apostasy. The people turn from the God of Abraham, Isaac, and Jacob as they worship false gods such as Baal. In this, they violate the first commandment (Exod 20:2-6; Deut 5:6-10). Step 2: God's punishment. God sends hardship upon the people, often by strengthening their enemies to conquer them. Step 3: the people's repentance. In their misery, the people reflect on their turning away from God and realize their mistake. Admitting their sin, they cry out to God for forgiveness and resolve to abide by God's laws. Step 4: God's reconciliation. God ends the people's misery, forgives their sins, and blesses them with new life.

Guided by their perceived "law" or fourfold cycle of history, the Deuteronomists edited the historical accounts that now make up the books of Deuteronomy, Joshua, Judges, 1 and 2 Samuel, and 1 and 2 Kings. Whenever possible, they described the sequence of events according to their perceived cycle of apostasy, punishment, repentance, and reconciliation. Consider, for instance, Judges 3:7-11 concerning Othniel, a tribal leader or "judge" in the late thirteenth century BC. According to the Deuteronomists, the people first violated the first commandment: "The Israelites did what was evil in the sight of the LORD, forgetting the LORD their God, and worshiping the Baals and the Asherahs" (Judg 3:7). Second, God sent evil upon the Israelites: "The anger of the LORD was kindled against Israel, and he sold them into the hand of King Cushan-rishathaim" (3:8). Third, after eight years of oppression, the people repented: "The Israelites cried out to the LORD" (3:9a). Given the people's conversion, God delivered them from their enemy: "The LORD raised up a deliverer for the Israelites, who delivered them, Othniel" (3:9b). When Othniel waged war against the people's oppressors, God "gave King Cush-rishathaim of Aram into his hand; and his hand prevailed over Cush-rishathaim" (3:10).

The Deuteronomists' view of God and human suffering fueled the Israelites' theology of divine retribution (Latin *retribuere,* "to give back"; see chap. 2). This theology holds that God does to us something comparable to what we do to God. God takes care of us when we love God. But when we turn away from God, God punishes us, tempering this punishment with mercy. As noted in chapter 2, the Deuteronomists held that God commanded Moses to speak of divine retribution: "See, I am setting before you today a blessing and a curse: the blessing, if you obey the commandments of the LORD your God that I am commanding you today; and the curse, if you do not obey the commandments of the LORD your God, but turn from the way that I am commanding you today, to follow other gods that you have not known" (Deut 11:26-27; cf. 30:15-18).

The book of Job challenges the theology of divine retribution (as we noted in chap. 2). Although Job's friends uphold the theology of divine retribution (Job 11:14-15), Job rejects it (13:23). In the end, God agrees with Job and upbraids the defenders of the theology of divine retribution: "My wrath is kindled against you and against your two friends; for you have not spoken of me what is right, as my servant Job has" (42:7).

C. *Suffering as God's Purifying Love*

At times, the biblical writers speak of God as though God were an athletic coach who makes demands on athletes for their own improvement. In this perspective, God imposes hardships on us in order to turn our attention from ourselves to God and to other people. God is intent on improving our personal character so that we learn selfless love similar to God's selfless love, agape. When this view is applied to the Israelites' tragedies in 597 BC and 586 BC, it teaches that God brought about the Babylonian exile in order to improve the Israelites' love as a jeweler purifies silver in a fire: "I have tested you in the furnace of adversity" (Isa 48:10).

In 742 BC the prophet First Isaiah received God's call to proclaim God's word to the people of Jerusalem. But after Isaiah told God that he lacked the selfless love required for this mission, he found himself being purified in God's presence (Isa 6:1-8): "I saw the Lord sitting on a throne, high and lofty." Surrounding God were angelic beings, "seraphs," who cried out, "Holy, holy, holy is the LORD of hosts." At this, the prophet exclaimed, "Woe is me! I am lost, for I am a man of unclean lips, and I live among a people of unclean lips; yet my eyes have seen the King, the LORD of hosts!" (6:5). An angel picked up a glowing ember in tongs, came to the prophet, and brought the burning coal to the prophet's mouth: "Now that this has touched your lips, your guilt has departed and your sin is blotted out" (6:7). After being seared by this ember, Isaiah heard God ask, "Whom shall I send, and who will go for us?" (6:8). Isaiah immediately responded, "Here am I; send me!" Having been purified by the burning ember, Isaiah was ready to proclaim God's message to Jerusalem's King Ahaz (735–715 BC).

Psalm 51, one of the penitential psalms, also conveys the view that God sometimes imposes suffering on us in order to rid us of our selfishness. The psalmist prays: "Have mercy on me, O God, according to your steadfast love; according to your abundant mercy blot out my transgressions. Wash me thoroughly from my iniquity and cleanse me from my sin" (Ps 51:1-2). How will God "blot out," "wash," and "cleanse" our sins? After acknowledging his guilt, the psalmist urges God, "Let me hear joy and gladness; let the bones that you have crushed rejoice" (51:8). In other words, the psalmist asks God to do what an athletic coach might do: place harsh demands on the psalmist so that the psalmist will be purified in selfless love in union with God: "Restore to me the joy of your salvation, and sustain in me a willing spirit" (51:12). God's cleansing will produce the psalmist's true "sacrifice": not a burnt offering in Jerusalem's temple but "a broken spirit; a broken and contrite heart, O God, you will not despise" (51:17). Speaking of suffering as purification, Pope John Paul II wrote that "suffering must serve for conversion, that is, for the rebuilding of goodness in the subject" (*Salvifici Doloris* 12).

In sum, what is the value of believing that God sends hardships upon us? The three views we've reviewed have the merit of assuring us that bad things happen to good people "for a reason" that is known to God. But these views also have the liability of implying that God possesses a dark side, an angry self, as well as a loving side, a merciful self.

III. God Allows Suffering

Some biblical writers speak of God allowing hardship to befall us. They acknowledge that God permits things to go wrong because God has bestowed freedom upon creation so that created beings can freely choose God. Bad things often occur, therefore, because we directly or indirectly bring these troubles on ourselves (e.g., by text messaging while we're driving a car). In this view, evil in creation has come about not because God intends it but because creatures have abused their God-given freedom. If this is the case, what does God "do" as we suffer? Does God stand on the sidelines and watch as though God were a silent spectator at a soccer game? Or does God somehow try to assist us when difficulties befall us?

A. Suffering as Caused by Evil

According to some biblical texts, God is continually engaged in a struggle with evil, even though God is the superior "force." Given its motif of a cosmic conflict between good and evil, this view is similar to the nonbiblical cosmology expressed in the movie series *Star Wars*. It differs, however, in that it holds that God as the LORD (see Exod

3:14-15) transcends every created being, even Satan, and hence that God could end evil if God chose to do this. Moreover, God's apparent inaction against evil is beyond human understanding. In this perspective, the Babylonian exile occurred because Satan was intent on turning the Israelites away from the LORD as these people endured the loss of Jerusalem's temple, the senseless deaths of their loved ones, their deportation, and their slavery in Babylon.

The biblical idea of Satan as a created, malevolent being is found in the first book of Chronicles (fifth century BC). According to the writer of Chronicles, King David deliberately disobeyed God's command that David not take a census of his soldiers. Why did David not listen to God's advice? "Satan stood up against Israel, and incited David to count the people of Israel" (1 Chr 21:1). Here, as in other postexilic biblical texts, "Satan" refers to a created, evil spirit who tempts human beings to rebel against God. (See chap. 2 concerning Satan as God's "accuser" in the divine court.) During the captivity in Babylon and then subsequently during the rise of Hellenism, the Israelites' understanding of evil was influenced by Babylonian and Greek mythologies concerning an evil being or rebellious gods. But, as mentioned, the people of Israel rejected the idea that Satan is God's equal.

The book of Wisdom (100 BC) presents Satan as a created, rebellious spirit. It holds that since God created us in God's "image" and "likeness" (Gen 1:26-27), God did not originally intend for human beings to undergo death: "God created us for incorruption, and made us in the image of his own eternity" (Wis 2:23). Interestingly, this postexilic view of death as a consequence of sin differs from the more ancient Israelite notion that death simply comes to all creatures (Gen 25:8; Job 42:17). In any case, according to the postexilic view, Satan brought about our mortality as a result of our sin. Alluding to the serpent in the story of Adam and Eve's sin (Gen 3:1-24), the Wisdom writer explains that "through the devil's envy death entered the world, and those who belong to his company experience it" (Wis 2:24). Implicit here is the biblical view that God and Satan struggle against one another, though they are not equals.

This idea of an ongoing conflict between God and evil has generated the biblical view that human suffering happens not because God intends it but because Satan seeks to poison creation. Similar to a virus that survives by sapping life out of what's healthy in us, so too evil is parasitic on what's good in creation. It twists something that is good in itself out of proportion in relation to the whole of life. For example,

King David misuses his sexuality and political power to seduce Bath-sheba (2 Sam 11:1–12:15). God is intent on remedying creation and also undoing evil and its sinister effects. In this salvific outreach, God is similar to a medical team using antibiotics to end an infection. We are the patients who try to cooperate with the "divine physician" in the struggle with evil. We ourselves are not bad or evil. Rather, we are afflicted with an "ailment," a disease that tries to pervert our goodness and our desire to live for God.[3]

Strong depictions of the struggle between God and evil emerge in the Bible's images of an apocalypse (Greek *apocalypsis*, "an unveiling"), which is history's final period when the battle between God and Satan is "unveiled," that is, breaks out as a flame can suddenly burst forth from smoking embers. In the apocalyptic perspective, world history will reach the "last" (Greek *eschatos*) age or the end-time when God will conquer Satan.

The book of Daniel (165 BC) is representative of apocalyptic literature. Written while the Jewish people in the Holy Land were being persecuted by the Seleucid (Hellenist Syrian) emperor Antiochus IV Epiphanes (175–163 BC), this book is meant to console and to inspire the Israelites amid their hardships, including their martyrdoms. The book of Daniel consists of stories about a fictitious figure Daniel and his companions, who are persecuted for their religious belief, remain faithful to God, and receive God's reward in the last age. (We'll discuss the book of Daniel again in chap. 5 concerning God's resurrection of the dead.)

As with all apocalyptic texts, the book of Daniel relies on symbols that seemingly concern a distant future but, in fact, specifically refer to people and events at the time when the book was written. We'll consider here only Daniel's vision of the "four great beasts," that is, the empires of the Babylonians, the Medes, the Persians, and the Greeks (Dan 7:1-28). Daniel refers in particular to Antiochus IV Epiphanes as the fourth beast's "little horn," or minor ruler (7:8). In his vision, Daniel witnesses the fall of Antiochus IV Epiphanes: "Thrones were set in place, and an Ancient One [God] took his throne." Wearing robes that were "white as snow," God sat on a throne that "was fiery flames, and its wheels were burning fire" (7:8-9). A trial commences, and the "arrogant words" of the "little horn" result in God's verdict against the Seleucid Empire: "The beast was put to death, and its body destroyed and given over to be burned with fire" (7:11). As the trial proceeds, "the rest of the beasts"—the empires of the Babylonians, the Medes, and the Persians—have "their dominion . . . taken away, but their lives were prolonged for a season and a time" (7:12).

In his vision, Daniel also sees the inauguration of God's new reign on earth: "I saw one like a human being coming with the clouds of heaven" (Dan 7:13). It is important to note that the expression "one like a human being" is synonymous with "one like a son of man." Moreover, the expression "son of man" may have two meanings. It may refer to God's glorified people, "Israel," in the last age. This corporate view of "son of man" makes sense in relation to the verse that "the holy ones of the Most High shall receive the kingdom and possess the kingdom forever" (7:18). Yet "son of man" may also mean a unique divine representative who establishes God's end-time. This apocalyptic leader receives from the "Ancient One" complete authority, that is, "dominion and glory and kingship, that all peoples, nations and languages should serve him" (7:13-14).

At the end of his vision, Daniel is once again told that although the "fourth beast" will prevail for a short while, its "dominion shall be taken away, to be consumed and totally destroyed" (Dan 7:26). Then God's last age will dawn: "The kingship . . . shall be given to the people of the holy ones of the Most High" (7:27).

What is a merit of the apocalyptic view of history, as evinced in the book of Daniel? Differentiating between God and Satan, it makes clear that God does not cause or even intend human misery. Whereas the prophets said that God directs divine anger against human beings who sin, the apocalyptic writers held that God sends the divine wrath upon Satan and Satan's minions. A second merit of the apocalyptic view is its claim that God asks us to assist God in undoing or at least holding at bay the work of evil in creation. A third merit is the recognition that God tolerates evil in creation because God remains committed to freedom in creation. As noted in chapter 2, if God desires that created beings love God, then God must leave created beings free to accept or to reject God. This reasoning leads, however, to an unresolved question: Even though the apocalyptic writers say that God will eventually destroy the evil powers, is it possible that God, life's Source and Goal, would choose to annihilate anyone or anything?

B. Suffering as the Result of Creation's Freedom

Our personal identity as individuals and as communities can be eroded if we undertake actions that go contrary to our values and commitments and hence contrary to our personal character. For example, during the American Civil War, President Abraham Lincoln temporarily suspended the law of habeas corpus so that the federal government could incarcerate likely saboteurs. But as he did so he was aware that he was jeopardizing the very reality for which he was fighting, namely, a democracy in which every human person has legal rights, including the right to a hearing before a magistrate before being imprisoned.

Similarly, are there some things that God simply will not do? Would God remain the LORD if God were to slay Satan? Wouldn't God lose God's "soul," so to speak, if God were to engage in a cosmic battle, in Armageddon (Rev 19:19)? Moreover, wouldn't it go contrary to the LORD's "personal character" if God were to use against Satan the tactics that Satan uses against God and God's people (e.g., deceit and violence)? If there are some things that God simply will not do, then God is seemingly at a disadvantage as God ceaselessly tries to bring good out of evil's effects and even to transform Satan.

Distinct from apocalyptic thought is the view that human suffering is the result of freedom in creation. Representative of this view is the Joseph narrative in Genesis 37–50. This literary composition is likely historical fiction. That is, on the one hand, it may refer to an actual individual, to a Hebrew man who held great power in Egypt during the Hyksos period (1650–1550 BC). On the other hand, this story includes many details and events that have little or no basis in ancient Egypt but reflect Hebrew nomadic life from the patriarchs Abraham, Isaac, and Jacob (1800 BC) to Moses (1250 BC). Moreover, the central figure in the Joseph narrative is not so much Joseph but the God of Abraham, Isaac, and Jacob. In Genesis 37–50, God is committed to Joseph and to the Hebrew people and thus often brings good out of evil on their behalf. The story likely originated as a literary whole in an oral tradition, received minor additions and modifications during its retellings, and was eventually written down with editorial revisions and additions by J, E, and P.

According to the narrator, Joseph was the youngest of Jacob's twelve sons and hence his father's favorite (Gen 37:3). For this reason, Joseph was rejected by his jealous older brothers, who sold him at the age of seventeen into slavery (37:28). Taken to Egypt, Joseph was enslaved to the pharaoh's chief steward, who came to prize Joseph's talents. Joseph did well because "the LORD was with Joseph" (39:2). Then, falsely accused of sexual misconduct (39:11-20), Joseph was imprisoned. However, he won the respect of his jailers; he again fared well because "the LORD was with him; and whatever he did, the LORD made it prosper" (39:23). Joseph eventually gained the respect of the pharaoh, who appointed Joseph to govern Egypt. After marrying, Joseph and his wife gave birth to two sons, Manasseh and Ephraim, whose names mean "God has made me forget all my hardship" and "God has made me fruitful" (41:50-52).

As Egypt's head of state, Joseph directed the Egyptians to store up their grain. Thus, "throughout the land of Egypt there was bread," even after famine struck the region (Gen 41:54). In search of food for their people, Joseph's brothers came to Egypt and asked to buy grain from Joseph, whom they did not recognize. Joseph sold them the grain without disclosing his identity. When Joseph was approached a second time by his brothers, he said to them, "I am Joseph. Is my father still alive?" But the brothers "could not answer him, so dismayed were they at his presence" (45:3). Joseph then explained, "I am your brother Joseph, whom you sold into Egypt. And now do not be distressed, or angry with yourselves, because you sold me here; for God sent me before you to preserve life" (45:4-5).

Soon afterward, Jacob traveled to Egypt and embraced his son Joseph (Gen 46:29). A few years later, Jacob died, and Joseph's brothers feared that Joseph would now punish them for their selling him into slavery. But Joseph told them: "Do not be afraid! Am I in the place of God? Even though you intended to do harm to me, God intended it for good, in order to preserve a numerous people, as he is doing today" (50:19-20). These powerful words succinctly express a fifth biblical view of the relationship between God and human suffering: although God allows evil to occur, God always finds ways to bring good out of evil. Upholding this view, St. Paul wrote that "all things work together for good for those who love God" (Rom 8:28).

This view of suffering as the result of creation's freedom sees that God did not intend the horrific suffering of the Israelites in the sixth century BC. Rather, throughout this tragedy, God sought to strengthen and guide the Israelites through their Babylonian captivity. Moreover, God eventually inspired the Persian ruler King Cyrus to liberate Babylon's enslaved Israelites, who out of gratitude eventually referred to Cyrus as God's "anointed," God's messiah (Isa 45:1).

IV. How Should We Face Hardship?

During the American Civil War, Abraham Lincoln wrote a letter of condolence to Fanny McCullough, whose father had died fighting for the Union. "It is with deep grief," he said, "that I learn of the death of your kind and brave Father." Having endured much suffering in his own life, the Lincoln stated a tragic truth: "In this sad world of ours, sorrow comes to all; and, to the young, it comes with the bitterest agony, because it takes them unawares. The older have learned to expect it."[4] This truth prompts the query, if sorrow is inevitable in our lives, how should we cope with it? This question receives at least three distinct answers in the Old Testament.

Answer 1: Act for Our Well-Being

According to the Old Testament, the greatest Israelite leaders often judged that God was calling them to overthrow their oppressors. In 1250 BC Moses led the Hebrews on their exodus, and Moses' successor, Joshua, subsequently conquered the people of Jericho (Josh 6). In 1125 BC Deborah marshaled the Israelite forces against the oppressive Canaanite army of General Sisera and destroyed them at the Wadi Kishon (Judg 4:1–5:31).

However, as we've already seen, the prophet Jeremiah rejected the decision by King Zedekiah and his advisors that they act against King Nebuchadnezzar's oppression of Judah and Jerusalem. Given Jeremiah's talk of acquiescing to the Babylonians, he was charged with disloyalty and accused of being a false prophet. As a result, he was incarcerated numerous times. Nevertheless, he was proven right by the course of events: Zedekiah's revolt was disastrous. In Jeremiah's view, the Babylonian exile shows that there are situations in which endurance rather than revolt is what God asks of us.

In contrast to Jeremiah's message, 1 Maccabees (written in about 90 BC) urges an aggressive response to hardship. This religious history recounts how Mattathias and his sons led a revolt in 168 BC against King Antiochus IV Epiphanes. In choosing to fight, they rejected the nonviolent resistance favored by other Jews, who were slaughtered by the king's soldiers. After hearing of this massacre, Mattathias and his friends "made this decision that day: 'Let us fight against anyone who comes to attack us on the sabbath day; let us not all die as our kindred died in their hiding places.'" Assembling an Israelite army, they fought against the Seleucid soldiers and forced them to withdraw from Judah. Then "Mattathias and his friends went around and tore down the [pagan] altars; they forcibly circumcised all the uncircumcised boys that they found within the borders of Israel. . . . They rescued the law out of the hands of the Gentiles and kings, and they never let the sinner gain the upper hand" (1 Macc 2:41, 45-46, 48).

The view that we should assert ourselves against life's setbacks possesses the merit of directing us to act for our well-being. It rightly directs us to exercise our self-agency in the face of peril. Yet it can imply at times that the end justifies the means. Was it right, for example, that Mattathias and his sons forcibly circumcised non-Jewish males? Moreover, what effect did killing people have upon Mattathias and his sons? As we assert ourselves against hardships, we must take care that our actions do not erode our personal character and hence our *salus*.

Answer 2: Engage in Lamentation

The Old Testament also witnesses to the religious practice of lamentation. That is, it directs us, when we're suffering, to cry out to God and even to address our anger to God. By doing so, we may find that we—like Job—will receive God's strength and guidance to endure our hardship. In this perspective, the book of Job is itself an extended lamentation in response to the Babylonian exile. As such, it reaches its highpoint when Job declares, "I had [previously] heard of you by the hearing of the ear, but now my eye sees you" (Job 42:5). During our suffering, lamentation can bring us closer to God.

Today the writer Elie Wiesel engages in lamentation in his books such as *Night*, his memoir of his survival at Auschwitz after his family was put to death there. Wiesel spoke of his deliberate lamentation when he was asked why God allowed the Shoah, the Holocaust: "I have not answered that question, but I have not lost faith in God. I have moments of anger and protest. Sometimes I've been closer to him for that reason."[5]

The Old Testament makes available to us numerous psalms of lamentation, some of which are individual laments, such as Psalms 3, 22, 51, 69, and 140, while others are communal laments, such as 12, 60, and 137.

Psalm 137 is noteworthy because it likely emerged during or shortly after the Babylonian exile: "By the rivers of Babylon—there we sat down and there we wept when we remembered Zion [Jerusalem]" (Ps 137:1). The Babylonians urged the Israelites, "Sing us one of the songs of Zion!" (137:3). But this was impossible: "How could we sing the Lord's song in a foreign land?" (137:4). The people longed for their homeland: "If I forget you, O Jerusalem, let my right hand wither!" (137:5). The Israelites prayed that God would punish the Babylonians: "O daughter Babylon, you devastator! Happy shall they be who pay you back what you have done to us!" (137:8).

The psalms of lamentation contain, to varying degrees, common elements: an address to God, a description of suffering, a cry for help, the cursing of the cause of the misery, confidence in God's help, an admission of innocence or guilt, the promise to thank God for divine assistance, and words of thanksgiving. The progression of these elements enables someone to move from feelings of despair and abandonment to trust in God and gratitude to God.[6]

Let's note the literary progression of lamentation in Psalm 22, the psalm that Jesus may have prayed as he was dying on the cross (Mark 15:14; see chap. 6). First, there are an address and a description: "My God, my God, why have you forsaken me?" (Ps 22:1). Next is the plea for help: "O my God, I cry by day but you do not answer" (22:2), and "To you they cried, and were saved; in you they trusted, and were not put to shame" (22:5). There also occurs the cursing of the cause of the misery: "For dogs are all around me; a company of evildoers encircles me" (22:16). The psalm expresses the victim's innocence: "It was you who took me from the womb; . . . . and since my mother bore me you have been my God" (22:9-10). It also gives voice to confidence in God's help: "But you, O Lord, do not be far away!" (22:19). During the last third of Psalm 22, the victim promises to thank God and then does so: "I will tell of your name to my brothers and sisters" (22:22). This trust in God builds: "All the ends of the earth shall remember and turn to the Lord" (22:27). Finally, the victim praises God: "Future generations will be told about the Lord, and proclaim his deliverance to a people yet unborn, saying that he has done it" (22:30-31).

In sum, as we endure hardships, psalms of lamentation can lead us to greater intimacy with God. As they express our dark emotions, they can lift us from despondency to trust in God.

Answer 3: Suffering as an Act of Atonement for Sin

According to the ancient Israelites, sin produces negative effects upon individuals and communities. It sets in motion destructive forces that continue even after the sinners themselves have repented of their misdeeds. For example, if a man in a burst of rage kills someone, he may admit his guilt and make an appropriate act of restitution. Yet, he may have ignited anger in the deceased's family, anger that drives a member of that family to harm someone else. Thus, there ensues a chain reaction of anger and harm, in short, of sin and its effects among many people. What will defuse this rage and its effects? According to the Old Testament, people who are suffering may pray that their hardships remove sin's negative impact among people so that these people may experience reconciliation or atonement ("at-one-ment") with God and one another.

The people of Israel came to see their suffering during the Babylonian exile as their atonement for sins. They expressed this understanding in the fourth of the Servant Songs (Isa 52:13–53:12). At the start, the song anticipates its end: "See, my servant shall prosper; he shall be exalted and lifted up" (52:13). Then it tells that this servant "grew up . . . like a root out of dry ground," that he "was despised and rejected by others, a man of suffering," and that "he has borne our infirmities" (53:2-4). As he suffered, he was "like a lamb that is led to the slaughter . . . [and] he did not open his mouth" (53:7). Although God is not named, God eventually speaks: "Out of his anguish he shall see light. . . . The righteous one, my servant, shall make many righteous, and he shall bear their iniquities" (53:11). Implicitly promising eternal life, God adds, "I will allot him a portion with the great . . . because he poured out himself to death, and was numbered with the transgressors." Finally, the song stresses that the servant's suffering will remove or eliminate sin's effects among people: "He bore the sin of many, and made intercession for the transgressors" (53:12). In other words, the servant's unjust hardship has brought about the community's reconciliation, enabling people to mature as interpersonal beings, as a "we."

This oracle from the Servant Songs possesses three ambiguities. (1) The "servant" could be an individual Israelite or the collective of enslaved Israelites. (2) The recipients of this atonement could be the enslaved Israelites alone or the entire people of Israel because some of the Israelites were not held captive in Babylon but remained in the Holy Land. Or the recipients could even be the entire human family, including the Babylonians themselves. (3) It is not clear whether God sent the suffering upon the "servant" or allowed this suffering to occur. The former view has a basis in 53:6: "The LORD has laid on him the iniquity of us all." Yet the latter view is conveyed in 53:3: "He was despised and rejected by others; a man of suffering and acquainted with infirmity."

These ambiguities do not need to be resolved here. It suffices to observe that the fourth Suffering Servant song teaches that we can dedicate our hardships for the removal of sin's obstacles to people's solidarity and their union with God. In doing this, we can adopt a constructive approach to the suffering we're enduring. Instead of passively reacting to our difficulties, we can adopt an active or creative attitude toward them.

The apocryphal or deuterocanonical book 4 Maccabees (written in about AD 40) attests that our suffering can be an act of atonement. This religious history of Jewish martyrs recounts that while the Jewish priest Eleazar was being put to death, he prayed aloud, "You know, O God, that though I might have saved myself, I am dying in burning torments for the sake of the law. Be merciful to your people, and let our punishment suffice for them. Make my blood their purification, and take my life in exchange for theirs" (4 Macc 6:27-29). That martyrdom can reconcile people with one another and with God is reiterated when it is observed that the Jews who died for their faith became, "as it were, a ransom for the sin of our nation. And through the blood of those devout ones and their death as an atoning sacrifice, divine Providence preserved Israel that had previously been mistreated" (17:21-22).

The view that our suffering could contribute to reconciliation or atonement may be difficult for us to understand. Nevertheless, this outlook has persisted in the Jewish and Christian communities. Indeed, it guides some people to relate in constructive ways to a terminal illness, a disability, depression, or unemployment. Since it highlights the potential constructive significance of seemingly meaningless hardship, it can enable people to bear their difficulties with such extraordinary faith, hope, and love that they profoundly heal the hearts, minds, and wills of people whom they do not even know.

We've seen that the Old Testament offers at least three responses to the question of how we should view hardship in our lives: act for our well-being, engage in lamentation, or suffer as an act of atonement. How do we know which answer is appropriate for us in a specific situation? We can turn to God in prayer. One prayer that may be helpful is "The Serenity Prayer," which is attributed to Reinhold Niebuhr: "God, grant me the serenity to accept the things I cannot change, the courage to change the things I can, and the wisdom to know the difference."

V. The Mystery of Human Suffering

As Romano Guardini was dying in 1968, he observed that since there is no fully adequate answer in this life to the question of human suffering, he hoped to receive God's explanation in the next life. He prayed that, after dying, he would be brought before God and then be permitted to ask, "Why, God, these fearful detours on the way to salvation; why the suffering of the innocent; why sin?" He was consoled by his expectation that God will eventually shed light on the mystery of God's relationship with us in our hardships.

Guardini knew, of course, that the Old Testament contains various forms of theodicy: suffering as God's wake-up call, as God's retribution, as God's purifying love, as caused by evil, and as the result of freedom. He was aware too that according to the Scriptures we can cope with hardship by acting against it, by engaging in lamentations, or by seeing it as an act of atonement.

At the same time, Guardini recognized that the Old Testament's diverse forms of theodicy implicitly witness to the fact that God's relationship to human suffering is a mystery; it is a complex, inexhaustible reality that we can increasingly understand but not fully fathom. The biblical writers sought to answer why bad things happen to good people. In their search for new insights, they relied on numerous and diverse images and ideas to shed light on the mystery. Yet they also recognized that human answers are always inadequate and provisional. Thus, the Bible ultimately leaves us speaking Job's words: "Therefore I have uttered what I did not understand, things too wonderful for me, which I did not know" (Job 42:3).

In 1968 Romano Guardini may have spoken with his visitors about an image concerning God and human suffering that he had discussed in 1963. In a meditation on divine wisdom, Guardini proposed that God "creates human existence as a tapestry in which every thread supports other threads and is simultaneously supported by them."[7] In other words, divine wisdom knits each of our lives into a tapestry and simultaneously weaves each of our tapestries into one unified tapestry of God's people and creation. During our earthly lives, we see only the back of this grand, divine weaving. That is, we observe only the partial threads, the knots, and the gaps in our lives and in human events. However, after our deaths, when we enter into God's presence, we will receive the gift of seeing the front of God's tapestry. We shall behold the exquisite beauty and coherence of God's weaving together of our lives. Guardini wrote:

At that moment the tapestry's great patterns will clearly stand out. Then too, we shall hear answers to our questions that received only partial answers or perhaps no answers during our lives, questions such as: Why? Why these hardships? What of these deprivations? Why did this occur and not that? All of these questions raised by life's injustices will be answered by divine wisdom—the wisdom that will have brought it about that the people and events of our lives did not simply occur by chance but have formed a coherent whole, a "world."[8]

Chapter 5

Hope
Actively Awaiting the Gift Fulfilled

J. R. R. Tolkien, the author of *The Lord of the Rings*, observed in 1939 that there exists a complementarity between fairy tales and the Bible. A fairy tale possesses "the Consolation of the Happy Ending." That is, it builds to a culminating point at which "sorrow and failure" yield to "the joy of deliverance." For example, although Cinderella is subservient to her stepmother and stepsisters for many years, she is eventually rescued by the prince and weds into royalty. A fairy tale ends with a reversal: the story of an impending catastrophe suddenly ends well so that it becomes, Tolkien said, a "eucatastrophe." (*Eu* in Greek means "good," as in "euphoria.") As a fairy tale moves from disaster to victory, it awakens in us our yearning for our lives to end well; it enlivens in us "the oldest and deepest desire, the Great Escape: the Escape from Death."[1]

The Bible complements fairy tales, Tolkien pointed out, because it attests that God will fully satisfy our deep-seated longing for "the Escape from Death." The Old Testament and the New Testament declare that God will "create new heavens and a new earth" in which "no more shall the sound of weeping be heard" (Isa 65:17, 19; Rev 21:1). In the last age, God will bring about the resurrection of the dead to eternal life (Dan 12:2). In fact, God has already "raised" Jesus Christ "on the third day in accordance with the scriptures" (1 Cor 15:4). Tolkien held that the gospels of Matthew, Mark, Luke, and John embrace "the essence of fairy stories." He writes, "The Birth of Christ is the eucatastrophe of Man's history. The Resurrection is the eucatastrophe of the story of the Incarnation. This story begins and ends in joy."[2] Thus, the Bible promises that God will fulfill what fairy tales ignite in us: "the joy of deliverance."

Tolkien's linking of fairy tales and the Bible provides a fruitful entry point into the biblical notion of hope with its vision of God's new creation. In the last age or end-time, God will bestow on God's people the fullness of salvation. Yet this vision contains two distinct forms of eschatology (Greek *eschatos*, "last," and *logos*, "study of"): prophetic eschatology and apocalyptic eschatology. As we'll see, the former is expressed in the book of Isaiah and the latter in the book of Daniel. Finally, the vision of God's new creation also generates the expectations for a "messiah" who will usher in this last age. According to Third Isaiah, this divinely "anointed" individual will wear "a helmet of salvation" and arrive in "Zion as Redeemer" (Isa 59:17, 20). However, this general expectation generated numerous differing images. That there existed no consensus in biblical Judaism concerning the identity or "job description" of a messianic figure is crucial for understanding the religious context in which Jesus of Nazareth undertook his public ministry during the first century AD.

I. The Biblical Notion of Hope

Some of us are born optimists, while others are natural pessimists. When optimists look at a glass of water, they immediately see the water and disregard the empty area. Yet when pessimists view the same glass of water, they focus on the empty area and neglect the water in the glass. Given their respective dispositions, optimists are creative in some situations though naïve in others, and pessimists are prudent some of the time but defeatist at other times. While optimists and pessimists approach life from opposite points, they can find common ground in hope. Hope is the middle way. It satisfies optimists because it highlights the strengths and their possibilities in a situation, and it attracts pessimists because it admits the weaknesses and their risks. In sum, hope can produce a realistic view of a situation along with an affirmation of what's valuable and possible.

A definition is in order. Hope is "the expectation of something desired," and "to hope for" is "to expect with desire."[3] This definition rightly recognizes hope's sense of uncertainty: that which is desired and expected will not automatically come about. Thus, hope unites desire, expectation, and uncertainty. In this, it transcends both optimism and pessimism. "To hope in" is "to trust, to have confidence in." Implicit in this definition is the sense of relying on someone else, of entrusting one's well-being or *salus* to another person or persons.

Now consider the distinction between humanistic hope and biblical hope. Humanistic hope is the expectation that women and men will eventually shape things for the best. It relies on and trusts in human persons, assuming that they possess the aspiration, ability, and will for what's best for everyone. In contrast, biblical hope relies primarily on God. As a fruit of theonomy, it regards God as the LORD, life's Source and Goal, in whom we trust and in relation to whom we relate to one another, ourselves, and creation as we live and act for what is possible. Thus, to possess biblical hope is "to wait for" and "to trust" God. The psalmist prays, "For you are my hope, O Lord; my trust, O God, from my youth" (Ps 71:5). Using "hope" as a divine name, the prophet Jeremiah exclaims, "O hope of Israel! O LORD! All who forsake you shall be put to shame; . . . they have forsaken the fountain of living water" (Jer 17:13). In short, biblical hope is the anticipation that God will bring us beyond all obstacles—even beyond evil, meaninglessness, and death—to the fullness of life in union with God.

Biblical hope relies on the Bible's narratives and testimonies about God's salvific presence to and action for God's people in the past. This reliance is evident when the psalmist sings, "Give thanks to the LORD, for he is good, for his steadfast love endures forever. . . . Then they cried to the LORD in their trouble, and he delivered them from their distress" (Ps 107:1, 6). The psalmist also recalls that God "sent signs and wonders into your midst, O Egypt, against Pharaoh. . . . For the LORD will vindicate his people, and have compassion on his servants" (Ps 135:9, 14).

Further, biblical hope arises from faith in God. This trust in God shows itself when Abram and Sarai heeded God's call to leave Haran and to travel to a land unknown to them, to Canaan: "Go from your country and your kindred . . . to the land that I will show you. . . . I will make you a great nation, and I will bless you" (Gen 12:1-2). They believed in God and thus had hope amid adversity, even with Sarah's barrenness. How could they become "a great nation" when they could not even conceive a child? Yet for God all things are possible; God rhetorically asked, "Is anything too wonderful for the LORD?" (18:14). Thanks to God's action, Sarah "conceived and bore Abraham a son in his old age, at the time of which God had spoken to him" (21:2). Almost two millennia later, St. Paul praised Abraham and Sarah because, "hoping against hope, they believed that [Abraham] would become 'the father of many nations'" (Rom 4:18).

Finally, biblical hope nurtures love of God, ourselves, others, and the earth. It disposed Moses to respond to God's call at the burning bush (Exod 3:10). Accepting his personal identity as given by God, Moses passionately acted for the well-being of the Israelites as he led them out of slavery, across the Red Sea, and through the Sinai desert to the Holy Land. Yet he acted not on his own strength but in response to God's initiatives. When he faced the Red Sea, he waited for God to open the waters: "The LORD will fight for you, and you have only to keep still" (14:14). As God did so, Moses led the Israelites "on dry ground through the sea" (14:29).

In sum, biblical hope actively awaits God's saving presence and action for our well-being. It directs us to trust God, and it simultaneously motivates us to look for, bring about, and pursue the opportunities and possibilities that God invisibly initiates for us. Moreover, biblical hope guides and strengthens us when we desire the "Great Escape" in the face of death. It rhetorically asks, "Is anything too wonderful for the LORD?" (Gen 18:14).

II. The Resurrection of the Dead

As Tolkien noted, fairy tales have happy endings: Little Red Riding Hood is pulled alive from the wolf's belly. Hansel and Gretel escape from the witch's cages and find their way home to their father's warm embrace. These happy endings are always contained within the world of the fairy tale; they do not tell of their characters going beyond death into a new reality. Yet, in Tolkien's words, they nonetheless stir up "the oldest and deepest desire, the Great Escape: the Escape from Death." And this "deepest desire" finds assurance of fulfillment in the Bible.

Biblical belief in God's resurrection of the dead came to explicit articulation beginning in the fourth century BC. Yet it did not fall from the sky, nor did it seep into the Israelites' consciousness from the neighboring religions. Belief that God lifts God's people out of death, the "Pit," emerged out of the biblical testimonies concerning God as the LORD, life's Source and Goal, who intends for people to attain the fullness of life. This conviction undergirds the creation narratives (Gen 1–2) and the stories of Abraham and Sarah (12–25). It runs through the narratives of the exodus that we considered in chapter 3. It also manifests itself in the biblical stories concerning Joseph and his brothers (37–50): Joseph survived slavery and rose to great influence in Egypt because "the LORD was with him" (39:3). This same belief in the Lord was voiced by the holy woman Hannah when she thanked God for enabling her to give birth to Samuel: "The LORD kills and brings to life; he brings down to Sheol and raises up" (1 Sam 2:6).

According to the Bible, the resurrection of the dead is the divine act in which God "raises" human persons in their entirety to a new mode of living forever in personal wholeness, in union with God, and in solidarity with other people and with creation. To put it another way, human persons will receive in heaven their full personal identities, their true countenances. Each of us will fully become the integrated "I," "we," and "doer" whom God envisioned at our births. Using Jesus' parable of the treasure in the field (Matt 13:44), we can say that, in raising us to eternal life, God will cherish us as the treasure for which God has purchased the field. Or, to change metaphors, in the last age God will work with each of us so that each will bring his or her potential chorus of voices into full harmony with all of the other choruses in the heavenly choir (Rev 5:13). In order to clarify the biblical notion of resurrection, we shall differentiate it from the notions of immortality and resuscitation.

A. Neither Immortality nor Resuscitation

Jews and Christians believe in much more than immortality (Latin *immortalis*, "not mortal," "exempt from death"). The notion of immortality arose within Greek thought. According to Socrates (d. 399 BC) and Plato (d. 347 BC), a human person's soul exists prior to his or her birth, continues through the individual's earthly existence, and survives after death. In the *Phaedo*, Socrates's disciple cites Socrates's words that the soul is "the immortal part" of us: "Our souls will exist [after death] somewhere in another world" (106E; 107A). He recalls too that Socrates sought to calm Crito and his friends after he, Socrates, was condemned to death by drinking hemlock. Socrates explained to his friends that they would not bury him when they buried his corpse. He—that is, his soul—would still be alive, for "when I have drunk the poison I shall remain with you no longer, but depart to a state of heavenly bliss" (*Phaedo*, 115D).[4] The language of immortality in Greek and Roman thought generates the view of us abiding as disembodied spirits or souls after death. Distinguishing between the "soul" and the "body," it regards the latter as a coat that we lug around in this life and then shed as we enter into the next life. Such an understanding of the human body, and implicitly of creation, goes contrary to the Bible's high regard for the human body and creation and hence contrary to the biblical view of life after death. In fact, the Bible does not distinguish between the "body" and the "soul."

Yet, according to the Bible, neither can God's resurrection of the dead be reduced to resuscitation (Latin *resuscitare*, "to stir up, to put into motion"). To resuscitate someone is to revive the individual from death or a coma so that he or she can resume earthly life until death. When a fairy tale tells of someone being restored to life—for example, Little Red Riding Hood or Sleeping Beauty—it is speaking of resuscitation. Of course, the Bible too includes accounts of resuscitation. For example, the prophet Elijah restored to earthly life the son of a widow in Zarephath (1 Kgs 17:8-24), and the prophet Elisha resuscitated the son of the woman in Shunem (2 Kgs 4:8-37). About eight hundred years after Elijah and Elisha, Jesus of Nazareth also resuscitated people. According to the gospels, he revived the daughter of Jairus (Mark 5:21-43), the slave of a Roman centurion in Capernaum (Luke 7:1-10), the son of a widow in Nain (Luke 7:11-17), and Lazarus of Bethany who "had already been in the tomb for four days" (John 11:1-44, 17). These restorations of deceased people to earthly existence are significant because they disclose God's commitment to give us *salus* in this world and also to bring us to the fullness of life in the new creation. But these resuscitations themselves are not resurrections.

The biblical notion of resurrection contains elements similar to the ideas of immortality and resuscitation, and yet it surpasses them. It resembles the idea of immortality in that it conveys the sense of the continuity of our personal journeys from this life into the next. But the notion of resurrection makes clear that the essence or identity of a human person is much more than a soul or spirit. It highlights that God's raising us to eternal life includes our personal existence as an embodied subject, a social being, and a self-agent. Further, the notion of resurrection is similar to the idea of resuscitation in that it clarifies the sacred character of our bodies and of creation. But it is dissimilar in that it emphasizes God's radical transformation of us as embodied persons to an entirely new mode of existence (see 1 Cor 15:44).

B. Resurrection

The resurrection (Latin *resurgere,* "to rise, to awaken") of a deceased human person is God's transformation of this human being in his or her embodied totality into transcendent life beyond death, meaninglessness, and evil. As the Jewish scholar Jon D. Levenson has observed, the Bible attests that God's resurrection of the dead will happen in the last age; it is "an eschatological event." The resurrection "is expected to occur in history but also to transform and redeem history and open on to a barely imaginable world beyond anything that preceded it."[5]

According to 2 Maccabees (written in about 100 BC), numerous Jews chose to be martyred at the hands of soldiers rather than to engage in the religious practices required in the Seleucid Empire. In doing so, they witnessed to their belief in God's resurrection of the dead. For example, 2 Maccabees 7:1-42 recounts that when a mother and her seven sons were awaiting martyrdom, they praised God and attested to the new life that God would bestow on them. The second son declared, "The King of the universe will raise us up to an everlasting renewal of life, because we have died for his laws" (2 Macc 7:9). Further, the fourth son said to his executioner, "One cannot but choose to die at the hands of men and to cherish the hope that God gives of being raised again by him. But for you there will be no resurrection to life" (7:14). Forced to watch her sons' torments, the mother "bore it with good courage because of her *hope* in the Lord" (7:20; italics added). Moreover, she assured her sons that "the Creator of the world, who shaped the beginning of humankind and devised the origin of all things, will in his mercy give life and breath back to you again, since you now forget yourselves for the sake of his laws" (7:23). When the mother saw her last son come before his executioner, she envisioned the "day" when God would reunite her with her seven sons. Thus, she exhorted the seventh son, "Accept death, so that in God's mercy I may get you back again along with your brothers" (7:29). Finally, the mother "died, after her sons" (7:41).

This remembrance of the martyrdom of the mother and her sons is meant to inspire its readers to remain faithful to God regardless of the personal cost. It clearly manifests the Jewish belief that God's resurrection of the dead will unite people with God, transform them as embodied persons, and bring them into communion with their loved ones.

The biblical understanding of God's resurrection of the dead comes to the fore as well in the book of Wisdom. Written during the first century BC, it includes a two-part account concerning the fate of someone (e.g., a whistle-blower) who pursues justice and truth. First, Wisdom 2:10-24 recounts that when a just or "righteous" person comes among us, "ungodly" people say, "Let us lie in wait for the righteous man, because he is inconvenient to us and opposes our actions" (Wis 2:12). Troubled by a just person's words, deeds, and personal presence, deceitful people say, "Let us test him with insult and torture" (2:19). They may even declare, "Let us condemn him to a shameful death, for, according to what he says, he will be protected [by God]" (2:20). Acting on their threats, evil people will torment and even murder a just or righteous person. But, according to the biblical writer, that is not the end of the story.

Let's pause for a moment and note that Wisdom 2:10-24 is similar to a story told by Plato. In Plato's *Republic*, book 2, Socrates tells Glaucon that a person who is just, not merely in appearance but in his or her very person, will be persecuted in any society. Agreeing with Socrates, Glaucon adds that "the just man will have to endure the lash, the rack, chains, the branding iron in his eyes, and finally, after every extremity of suffering, he will be crucified" (361E).[6] Although Socrates and Glaucon do not talk here about the immortality of the souls of the people who are just, they surely imply it. In their view, after a just person is ridiculed and put to death, the person's soul leaves the body, passes through death, and abides in eternal life.

Consider again the book of Wisdom. Although the book's writers adopt words such as "soul" and "immortality," they use these terms to speak about God's resurrection of the just or righteous. According to Wisdom 3:1-9, after their deaths, "the souls of the righteous are in the hand of God, and no torment will ever touch them" (Wis 3:1). Their deaths were "thought to be a disaster, and their going from us to be their destruction; but they are at peace" (3:3). Indeed, "their hope is full of immortality" (3:4), and God "found them worthy of himself" (3:5). In the last age, they "will shine forth, and will run like sparks through the stubble" (3:7). Having trusted in God, they "will understand truth," and they "will abide with [God] in love, because grace and mercy are upon his holy ones, and [God] watches over his elect" (3:9).

In its literary context, Wisdom 2:10–3:9 conveys a belief in God's resurrection of the dead that is similar to the view expressed in 2

Maccabees 7:1-42. In this vein, Jon Levenson writes that the Bible's version of immortality "is quite close to resurrection." It is not the notion of "an immaterial and imperishable soul." Rather, biblical talk of immortality refers to "a painfully vulnerable 'life' . . . that God will 'take' or redeem . . . whereas others less worthy will descend into Sheol without hope."[7]

Finally, the psalms repeatedly say that God is our "salvation" and gives us the fullness of life. Consider these verses: "You show me the path to life. In your presence there is fullness of joy" (Ps 16:11). "He brought me out into a broad place; he delivered me, because he delighted in me" (Ps 18:19). "Even though I walk through the darkest valley, I fear no evil; for you are with me; your rod and your staff—they comfort me" (Ps 23:4). "I believe that I shall see the goodness of the LORD in the land of the living" (Ps 27:13). "For great is your steadfast love toward me; you have delivered my soul from the depths of Sheol" (Ps 86:13). God "will deliver you from the snare of the fowler and from the deadly pestilence. . . . [God says,] With long life I will satisfy them, and show them my salvation" (Ps 91:3, 16). "For you have delivered my soul from death, my eyes from tears, my feet from stumbling. I walk before the LORD in the land of the living" (Ps 116:8-9). "I shall not die, but I shall live, and recount the deeds of the LORD" (Ps 118:17).

These texts attest to the Israelites' hope in God and, specifically, to their hope in God's resurrection of the dead. In light of their experiences of God as LORD, as "the One who causes [us] to be," the people of Israel hoped that God would somehow bring them to life beyond death. Moreover, they envisioned God establishing a new creation in God's end-time.

III. The Coming of God's Last Age

As Tolkien noted, a true fairy tale always reaches a happy ending (even in the movie *Shrek*). Although it unfolds as a tale headed toward a catastrophe, it ultimately recounts a eucatastrophe, a potential disaster that ends well. The Bible too communicates an overarching narrative in which creation and history culminate in a happy ending, the last age or end-time, when God will be united with God's people on Mount Zion, Jerusalem. Even though the Israelites' neighboring peoples usually held circular views of life, the people of Israel cherished a linear view of creation and history. That is, they believed that history as well as creation had a beginning (Gen 1:1; 2:4b) and that they themselves as God's people had a starting point: God's covenant with Abraham and Sarah (12:1-3). Further, they saw that God had subsequently renewed the people's lives and God's covenant with them as God issued fresh calls to individuals such as Moses, Deborah, and David (Exod 3; Judg 4; 2 Sam 7). In sum, the Israelites saw themselves as participants in God's story or drama of creation and history.

This linear sense of creation and history fueled the question of the earthly drama's endpoint. If the story has a beginning and an unfolding, will it have a happy ending? Yes, it will, the biblical writers said. God will bring about a new creation in which "steadfast love and faithfulness will meet; righteousness and peace will kiss each other" (Ps 85:10). But this answer prompts a further question: Will the drama of creation and history have an ending that unfolds out of what had preceded it, as a renewed vine appears after its pruning (Isa 5:1-7)? Or would the happy ending come about after a divine disruption, similar to God's sending the Flood at the time of Noah (Gen 6:1-8)?

These questions about the culminating point of creation and history gave rise to two distinct, though interrelated, views concerning the arrival of God's last age. During the conquest of the northern kingdom by the Assyrians in 722 BC, there began what is now called "prophetic eschatology." About five hundred years later, during the persecution of Jews in the Seleucid Empire, there flourished what is now termed "apocalyptic eschatology."

A. Prophetic Eschatology

The Israelite prophets promoted the view that God will eventually act in history so that the people of Israel will form a lasting community of blessing, reminiscent of the best aspects of King David's reign or kingdom. This community will be a realm that is in continuity with and yet a transformation of creation and history. This prophetic view of history rests on the prophets' understanding that God sends suffering upon the chosen people in order to bring about their repentance (see chap. 4), and it maintains that God will eventually establish a new community of "steadfast love and faithfulness" (Ps 85:10). In this new community, the New Jerusalem, God's people will live in union with God, in communion with one another, in peace with their neighbors, and in harmony with creation. Prophetic eschatology contains, however, an ambiguity. It speaks of God's renewal of life within creation, and yet it simultaneously implies a transformation of life beyond death. Let's consider the testimonies of the prophets Amos, Hosea, Second Isaiah, Ezekiel, and Haggai.

The prophet Amos (eighth century BC) was an early proponent of prophetic eschatology. After the Assyrians conquered the Israelites in the northern kingdom in 722 BC, Amos declared that the people were enduring "the day of the LORD" (Amos 5:18). God was passing judgment on them because of their sins, in particular because of their social injustice (8:4). But, Amos said, God would eventually establish a new community. God had promised Amos, "I will restore the fortunes of my people Israel, and they shall rebuild the ruined cities and inhabit them; they shall plant vineyards and drink their wine, and they shall make gardens and eat their fruit" (9:14). Here, prophetic eschatology explicitly concerns the renewal of God's people within creation.

The prophet Hosea, a contemporary of Amos, also preached that God had sent the Assyrian oppression in 722 BC upon the Israelites in the northern kingdom in order to bring about their conversion. According to Hosea, "The LORD has an indictment against the inhabitants of the land. There is no faithfulness or loyalty, and no knowledge of God in the land" (Hos 4:1). Hosea promised that God was confident that the hardship would have beneficial results: "In their distress, they will beg my favor: 'Come, let us return to the LORD; for it is he who has torn, and he will heal us'" (5:15–6:1). The people's *metanoia* would lead, Hosea promised, to God's gift of the fullness of life: "After two days [God] will revive us; on the third day, he will raise us up, that we may live before him" (6:2). While this statement explicitly expresses the expectation that God will restore Israel in history, it also conveys the fuller sense or deeper meaning that God will bring about God's resurrection of the dead.

The book of Isaiah (chaps. 1–39) contains the words of the prophet First Isaiah, who ministered in Jerusalem from 740 to 701 BC. During these four decades, the Israelites' southern kingdom had to cope with the impact of the war between its neighbors Syria and Ephraim (734–732 BC) and also with the likelihood of being conquered by Assyria. Amid these difficulties, First Isaiah counseled the Israelites that they would survive and have a bright future if they would undergo a religious and moral renewal. Isaiah declared, "The ox knows its owner, and the donkey its master's crib; but Israel does not know [its God], my people do not understand" (Isa 1:3). Yet, according to the prophet, if the people would repent and return to God, then God would bring about their national rebirth: "In days to come, the mountain of the LORD's house [i.e., Jerusalem's temple] shall be established as the highest of the mountains, and shall be raised above the hills; all nations shall stream to it." Then God "shall judge between the nations," and "shall arbitrate for many peoples; they shall beat their swords into plowshares, and their spears into pruning hooks." The world will be at peace: "Nation shall not lift up sword against nation, neither shall they learn war any more" (2:2-4). While First Isaiah's words were likely meant to apply to an event in the immediate future, they also imply a deeper significance concerning God's intention for creation and history's "happy ending."

The book of Isaiah (chaps. 40–55) includes of the teachings of Second Isaiah, the prophet who ministered to the Israelites after the fall of Jerusalem and during the Babylonian exile (586–538 BC). Second Isaiah nurtured the enslaved Israelites' hope that God would liberate them and bring them back to Jerusalem, where they would establish the new Israel. According to Second Isaiah, God had announced, "I am about to do a new thing; now it springs forth, do you not perceive it? (Isa 43:19). God had even declared, "Go out from Babylon, flee from Chaldea, declare this with a shout of joy . . . ; say, 'The LORD has redeemed his servant Jacob!'" (48:20). According to Second Isaiah, "The ransomed of the LORD shall return, and come to Zion with singing; everlasting joy shall be on their heads" (51:11). While these words foretell God's liberation of the Israelites in 538 BC, they also attest to much more, namely, to God's end-time for creation and history.

The book of Isaiah also contains two distinct passages with views of God's radical intervention in history that exceed the explicit scope of prophetic eschatology and thus foreshadow apocalyptic eschatology. These texts employ imagery of God transforming creation and history into a wholly new creation and raising God's faithful people to communal life beyond death in union with God.

The first of these passages is Isaiah 24–27, known as the Apocalypse of Isaiah. According to these chapters, God will bring about a wholly new life for the people who have died and those who are suffering. God states: "Your dead shall live, their corpses shall rise; O dwellers in the dust, awake and sing for joy! For your dew is a radiant dew, and the earth will give birth to those long dead" (Isa 26:19).

The second of the passages that moves toward an apocalyptic eschatology is Isaiah 56–66, a collection of teachings attributed to Third Isaiah, the prophet who ministered in Jerusalem after the Babylonian exile. These inspiring chapters express three ideas pertinent to our discussion. First, God has initiated a new state of affairs for the people of Israel: "Arise, shine; for your light has come, and the glory of the LORD has arisen upon you. . . . Nations shall come to your light, and kings to the brightness of your dawn" (Isa 60:1, 3). Second, God has commissioned a prophet of the last age to bring healing to everyone. This "anointed one" or "messiah" states, "The spirit of the Lord GOD is upon me, because the LORD has anointed me; he has sent me to bring good news [i.e., gospel] to the oppressed, to bind up the brokenhearted, to proclaim liberty to the captives, and release to the prisoners; to proclaim the year of the LORD's favor, and the day of vengeance of our God; to comfort all who mourn" (61:1-2; cf. Luke 4:16-21).

Third, according to Third Isaiah, God will renew all people, non-Jews as well as Jews. God has declared, "For I am about to create new heavens and a new earth. . . . I will rejoice in Jerusalem, and delight in my people; no more shall the sound of weeping be heard in it, or the cry of distress" (Isa 65:17, 19). Having enlivened the community of Jerusalem, God will then draw all people to participate in this new reality. According to Third Isaiah, God has said, "I am coming to gather all nations and tongues; and they shall come and see my glory, and I will set a sign upon them" (66:18-19a). Moreover, this new state of affairs will not perish, for God has promised, "For as the new heavens and the new earth, which I will make, shall remain before me, says the LORD; so shall your descendants and your name remain. . . . All flesh shall come to worship before me, says the LORD" (66:22-23). Third Isaiah may have had in mind an event that would occur in his lifetime, but he crafted such powerful words that his images evoke a sense that God's last age will be a radically new reality of joyous life.

The prophet Ezekiel assured the Israelites during the Babylonian exile that God would bring about their renewal in Jerusalem. Moreover, Ezekiel used imagery that conveys too a fuller sense or deeper meaning concerning God's resurrection of the dead. According to the prophet, God led him into the desert where deceased Israelites' dry bones lay. God instructed the prophet to speak these words over the bones: "O dry bones, hear the word of the LORD. Thus says the Lord GOD to these bones: I will cause breath to enter you, and you shall live" (Ezek 37:4-5).

Moreover, God said to Ezekiel: "Mortal [son of man], these bones are the whole house of Israel. They say, 'Our bones are dried up, our hope is lost, and we are cut off completely.' Therefore prophesy, and say to them, Thus says the Lord GOD: I am going to open your graves, and bring you up from your graves, O my people; and I will bring you back to the land of Israel" (37:11-12). In proclaiming his vision, Ezekiel himself may have specifically anticipated God's national renewal of the Israelites. Yet his words communicate much more: they tell of God's resurrection of the dead in the last age.

The prophet Haggai announced in 520 BC that God was intent on restoring the Israelite community in Jerusalem and that central to this renewal was the rebuilding of Jerusalem's temple. According to Haggai, God's message was straightforward: "Go up into the hills and bring wood and build the house [i.e., temple], so that I may take pleasure in it and be honored, says the LORD" (Hag 1:8). Moreover, God would bless the Israelites through their leader Zerubbabel, a descendant of King David. Haggai passed on God's word to Zerubbabel: "I am about to shake the heavens and the earth, and to overthrow the throne of kingdoms. . . . I will take you, O Zerubbabel my servant, son of Sheal-tiel, says the LORD, and make you as a signet ring; for I have chosen you, says the LORD of hosts" (Hag 2:21-23). Haggai's foretelling of a new community with its divinely anointed leader conveys not only God's promise to restore postexilic Jerusalem but also God's promise to establish the New Jerusalem in God's end-time.

From 740 to 520 BC, the prophets Amos, Hosea, First Isaiah, Second Isaiah, Third Isaiah, Ezekiel, and Haggai assured the people of Israel that while God had sent suffering upon them, God would eventually send blessings upon them. God, the vinedresser, prunes the vine in order to remove harmful foliage and to foster fruitful growth (Isa 5:1-7). This message of hope included at least four specific themes. First, God would bring about their rebirth as a people in history and beyond time and space as we know them. Second, the people would encounter God in their new community, centered in a transformed Jerusalem, Mount Zion. Third, God would invite non-Jews as well as Jews into the New Jerusalem. Fourth, this new reality would come about through the leadership of God's messiah, God's anointed one.

It's important that we pursue this fourth theme concerning God's messiah. But before doing so, let's consider the apocalyptic eschatology that emerged after the prophetic eschatology.

B. Apocalyptic Eschatology

The representatives of an apocalyptic view of history held that God chose "to unveil" (*apokaluptein* in Greek) to them God's secret intention for the future. According to this divine disclosure or revelation, God will eventually disrupt creation and history when God defeats Satan in a final battle. Then God will undertake the Last Judgment and transform the cosmos into the new creation. These convictions are expressed in the book of Joel, the book of Daniel, and also in extrabiblical (pseudepigraphal) texts in Jewish literature—for example, in 1 Enoch. Whereas prophetic eschatology holds that God sends or allows evil to inflict suffering on God's people, apocalyptic eschatology assumes that God has never intended evil but has permitted it, struggles against it, and will eventually put an end to it.

The book of Joel, written in about 400 BC, announces that "the day of the LORD is near, and as destruction comes from the Almighty it comes" (Joel 1:15). On this day, fire will devour the fields and the trees (1:19). Preparing for this event, God urges the people, "Return to me with all your hearts . . . ; rend your hearts and not your clothing. Return to the LORD, your God, for he is gracious and merciful, slow to anger, and abounding in steadfast love, and relents from punishing" (2:12-13). Yet God will surely have a Day of Judgment: "The sun shall be turned to darkness, and the moon to blood, before the great and terrible day of the LORD comes." However, God will save "everyone who calls on the name of the LORD" (3:31-32). Indeed, God will bless all people who turn to God: "Then afterward I will pour my spirit on all flesh; your sons and your daughters shall prophesy, your old men shall dream dreams, and your young men shall see visions" (2:28; cf. Acts 2:1-13).

As noted in chapter 4, the book of Daniel (second century BC) imparts an apocalyptic vision of the end-time: God, "the Ancient One," appears on his throne of "fiery flames" (Dan 7:9) and judges "the beasts," the world's four corrupt empires, including the last beast's ruler, Antiochus IV Epiphanes. This beast "was put to death, and its body destroyed and given over to be burned with fire," and the other beasts were stripped of "their dominion," though they were allowed to live "for a season and a time" (7:11-12). There appears "one like a human being [a son of man]" who comes before "the Ancient One," who gives him "dominion and glory and kingship, that all peoples, nations, and languages should serve him" (7:13-14).

The book of Daniel explicitly speaks about God's resurrection of the dead (Dan 12:1-3). In his vision Daniel is told, "At that time Michael, the great prince, the protector of your people, shall arise. There shall be a time of anguish. . . . But at that time your people shall be delivered" (12:1). Then will come the moment of resurrection and judgment. "Many of those who sleep in the dust of the earth shall awake, some to everlasting life, and some to shame and everlasting contempt. Those who are wise shall shine like the brightness of the sky, and those who lead many to righteousness, like the stars forever and ever" (12:2-3).

1 Enoch (also called the Ethiopic Book of Enoch), which was written from 200 BC to AD 100, offers another apocalyptic view of God's last age. According to book 1, God unveiled the future to Enoch, a righteous Jew: "The God of the universe, the Holy Great One, will come forth from his dwelling. And from there he will march upon Mount Sinai and appear . . . with mighty power." All who behold this event shall be filled with "great fear and trembling," and "all that is upon the earth shall perish." Then God shall pass "judgment upon all, (including) the righteous," to whom God will grant peace. "He will preserve the elect, and kindness shall be upon them." However, God "will destroy the wicked ones and censure all flesh on account of everything that they have done, that which the sinners and the wicked ones committed against him." Book 1 also tells of the fall of the angels, of Enoch's efforts to save them, including Azazel, a demonic figure (see Lev 16:8), and of Enoch's tour of the earth, Sheol, and Jerusalem at "the center of the earth."[8]

In sum, apocalyptic eschatology—in the books of Joel, Daniel, and 1 Enoch—foretells the "day" when God will step into history, stop business as usual, and initiate God's last age. God will bring a transformation of creation and history that will far surpass God's sending of the flood and saving of Noah in the ark (Gen 6:1-8). In this "event," God will raise the dead to life and judge between the righteous and the wicked, welcoming the former among God's new people in Zion and sending the latter to "everlasting contempt" (Dan 12:2). Moreover, God will destroy the rule of Satan (1 Enoch, bk. 1).

IV. Expectations for God's Messiah

While the ancient Israelites agreed that God would inaugurate the last age by sending a special figure, they differed concerning the character and role of this emissary. They frequently spoke of this figure as a messiah, an anointed one. This title "messiah" is derived from *mashiach* in Hebrew, which in Greek is *christos*. The term emerged from the Israelites' practice of anointing with oil a newly appointed king (Judg 9:8-15); for example, the elders anointed David as king (2 Sam 5:3). An anointing with oil also occurred during the investiture of a priest (Lev 4:3); for example, Moses anointed Aaron to be Israel's first priest (Exod 29:7). Finally, a literal or figurative anointing with oil sometimes happened with a prophet (Isa 61:1); for example, Elijah "anointed" Elisha when he "threw his mantle over him" (1 Kgs 19:6, 19). As the people of Israel imagined the in-breaking of God's last age, they extended the image of a king, a priest, and a prophet as God's anointed one to God's emissary or representative in this end-time. As noted earlier, Third Isaiah held that God's messiah would "come to Zion as Redeemer" (Isa 59:20). That said, there were differing views of the specific identity and role of this *mashiach*, this *christos*. Let us consider five motifs concerning God's anointed one and also discuss the motif of a martyr.

First, the motif of the king-messiah takes its bearings from the figure of King David, and it is anchored in God's promise to David: "I will raise up your offspring after you, who shall come forth from your body, and I will establish his kingdom. . . . I will be a father to him, and he shall be a son to me" (2 Sam 7:12, 14). Indeed, this anointed one would be, in some sense, God's son, for God had declared, "You are my son; today I have begotten you" (Ps 2:7). Moreover, God would make this Davidic-messiah a powerful king: "You shall break them with a rod of iron, and dash them in pieces like a potter's vessel" (Ps 2:9). God would empower this messiah to rule from God's throne: "Sit at my right hand till I make your enemies your footstool" (Ps 110:1). Yet, according to First Isaiah, this king-messiah would primarily govern not by his military might but by his personal authority: "For a child has been born for us, a son is given to us; authority rests upon his shoulders; and he is named Wonderful Counselor, Mighty God, Everlasting Father, Prince of Peace" (Isa 9:6).

Second, the figure of a priest-messiah arose from the image of the priest Aaron, who accompanied Moses into God's presence for the ratification of the Mosaic covenant (Exod 24:1). This expectation of a divinely appointed priest gained strength from biblical testimony concerning Melchizedek, the pre-Israelite priest and king who blessed

Abraham (Gen 14:18-20). Also, King David seemingly spoke in song of a priest-ruler similar to Melchizedek who would be superior to David himself: "The Lord has sworn and will not change his mind, 'You are a priest forever according to the order of Melchizedek'" (Ps 110:4; cf. Zech 6:9-14).

Third, along with the motifs of king-messiah and priest-messiah, there developed the image of a <u>prophet-messiah</u>. In response to Moses' question about his successor for the Israelites, God assured Moses, "I will raise up for them a prophet like you from among their own people; I will put my words in the mouth of the prophet, who shall speak to them everything that I command" (Deut 18:18). The prophet Malachi (fifth century BC) fueled this expectation of God's anointed one being a prophetic figure, perhaps even a Moses or an Elijah (Mal 4:4, 5). According to Malachi, God had said, "See, I am sending my messenger to prepare the way before me, and the Lord whom you seek will suddenly come to his temple." Like Moses and Elijah, this "messenger" will surely come "like a refiner's fire and like fuller's soap." He will purify and cleanse God's people. "But who can endure the day of his coming, and who can stand when he appears?" (3:1-3).

A fourth view of God's anointed one emerged from the book of Daniel's vision of the "son of man." As discussed above, after "the Ancient One" passed judgment on the four "beasts" (Dan 7:9-13), there appeared "one like a human being," that is, "one like a son of man," who arrived "with the clouds of heaven." This "son of man" came before God and "was given dominion and glory and kingship, that all peoples, nations, and languages should serve him" (7:14). In chapter 4 we noted that "son of man" may refer both to the collective people of Israel and to an individual person. Referring to Israel as a people, it means that in the last age God will appoint God's faithful people to rule the earth. Referring to an individual figure, "son of man" means God's anointed one who inaugurates God's end-time. It has this specific sense in 1 Enoch (chaps. 37–51). Building on Daniel 7:14, Enoch is told in a vision that "this Son of Man whom you have seen is the One who would remove the kings and the mighty ones from their comfortable seats and the strong ones from their thrones. . . . For they do not extol and glorify him, and neither do they obey him, the source of their kingship" (chap. 46).[9]

Fifth, there arose the image of a shepherd-messiah. In the fifth century BC, the prophet Zechariah envisioned God appointing a leader for

Israel who would rule by means of his personal charisma and genuine care for God's people: "Lo, your king comes to you; triumphant and victorious is he, humble and riding on a donkey. . . . He will cut off the chariot from Ephraim and the warhorse from Jerusalem; the battle now shall be cut off, and he shall command peace to the nations" (Zech 9:9-10). Indeed, he would govern as a good shepherd tends the sheep: "On that day the LORD their God will save them for they are the flock of his people; for like the jewels of a crown they shall shine on his land" (9:16). However, this shepherd-messiah would be killed by his people, who had turned against him (13:7). But afterward, when the people "look on the one whom they have pierced, they shall mourn for him, as one mourns for an only child, and weep bitterly over him, as one weeps over a firstborn" (12:10).

This fifth motif of a shepherd-messiah who would suffer implicitly points beyond itself to the image of a martyr. To be sure, the people of Israel respected their martyrs and held that their suffering could cleanse people of the effects of their sin. As we saw in chapter 4, they realized after the Babylonian exile that God could commission someone or even a group of people to undergo hardship for the well-being of all people. The fourth Servant Song attests, "But he was wounded for our transgressions, crushed for our iniquities; upon him was the punishment that made us whole, and by his bruises we are healed" (Isa 53:5). It was accepted, therefore, that martyrs could reconcile people with God through their suffering and death. But it was not anticipated that God's anointed one would have a job description that included martyrdom. No one expected that God's messiah would be a martyr, that the *christos* would be a "suffering servant" whose dying would bring atonement or reconciliation for God's people.

Let's sum up. By the first century AD, the people of Israel held at least five motifs of God's anointed one: king-messiah, priest-messiah, prophet-messiah, son-of-man–messiah, and shepherd-messiah. Also, they prized the image of the martyr, but they did not imagine God sending them a martyr-messiah.

Given this spectrum of views, first-century Jews could not agree on the identity and role of God's anointed one. In particular, they were unsure what to make of Jesus of Nazareth. At times, he spoke and acted with the authority of King David's successor. At other times, he seemed similar to Moses and Elijah or similar to Zechariah's shepherd-messiah. Yet he also referred to himself as the "Son of Man." Most shocking of all was that he spoke of his impending martyrdom. But how could Jesus be both God's messiah and God's martyr? Peter rightly identified Jesus as "the Messiah." But when Peter refused to link "messiah" and "martyr," he was abruptly reprimanded by Jesus: "Get behind me, Satan! For you are setting your mind not on divine things but on human things" (Mark 8:29, 33).

The Old Testament envisions the story of creation and history, including our lives, having a happy ending. It imparts hope that God will bring about God's last age. In its uplifting vision, the Old Testament addresses our deep-seated longing for what Tolkien called "the Great Escape: the Escape from Death." Is this basic human desire for eternal life merely wishful thinking? If so, ought we to ignore the fairy tales that enliven our yearning for *salus*? The Bible's answer is that God will surely fulfill our hearts' "oldest and deepest desire," our yearning for God's new creation. In short, God's story of creation and salvation is a eucatastrophe.

Further, the New Testament attests that God has already inaugurated God's last age. It witnesses to the "Good News" that God's reign is now secured in human affairs because of Jesus, God's anointed one, the Christ. This Good News, or Gospel, is anchored in the ancient proclamation or kerygma "that Christ died for our sins in accordance with the scriptures, and that he was buried, and that he was raised on the third day in accordance with the scriptures, and that he appeared to Cephas, then to the twelve" (1 Cor 15:3-5). Jesus is indeed the Christ, for he has overcome evil, meaninglessness, and death, and he has opened the way for all people to the fullness of God's gift of *salus*. In light of Jesus' life, death, and resurrection, Christians exclaim what God rhetorically asked concerning the birth of Abraham and Sarah's son Isaac: "Is anything too wonderful for the LORD?" (Gen 18:14). And, with Jesus, we declare: "Abba, Father, for you all things are possible" (Mark 14:36a).

Chapter 6

Jesus Christ
God's Gift and Our Yes

During the last fifty years, self-proclaimed prophets—such as Charles Manson, Jimmy Jones, and David Koresh—have lured lonely people into their web and then taken control of their followers' money, sexuality, and psyches. These narcissistic "religious" figures spoke often about themselves and about their alleged special ties with God. Some of them even implied that they were successors to Jesus.

Unlike these self-designated "messiahs," Jesus Christ said little about himself; he was not a narcissist. Also, not ensnaring his followers, Jesus released them from whatever or whoever enchained them, such as an infirmity, a demon, loneliness, or even death. Further, he empowered them for personal individuation in relation to him. In all this, he left them free to walk away from him as the rich young man did, to betray him as Judas did, and to deny knowing him as Peter did (Mark 10:17-22; 14:43-45, 66-72).

What was Jesus' message if it was not about himself? Jesus proclaimed the "Good News" or "Gospel" (Greek, *eu,* "good," + *angélion,* "news") about God's gift to us and about our appropriate response to this divine gift. Jesus announced, "The time is fulfilled, and the kingdom of God has come near; repent, and believe in the good news" (Mark 1:15; Matt 4:17; Luke 4:18, 44; John 3:5). In communicating this Good News, Jesus stood in the tradition of the prophet Second Isaiah (Isa 40:9; 41:27; 52:7) and the prophet Third Isaiah (Isa 61:1), both of whom announced the gospel that God, motivated by steadfast love, would free God's people from oppression and give them the fullness of life.

Notice that Jesus explicitly proclaimed God's gift of salvation and our yes to this divine offer. Although he conveyed much about himself, he left it to his post-Easter disciples to identify him as God's Son and the Savior of all people (Rom 1:2-3; 1 Cor 15:3-5). In response to the risen Christ and to the Holy Spirit, the apostles and disciples confessed that Jesus is the Christ (John 20:31; Acts 2:36). In this way, the apostles and disciples after Easter made explicit what Jesus left implicit. The church's Gospel or Good News concerns Jesus Christ as well as the coming of God's kingdom and our *metanoia* in response to God's kingdom and to the Lord Jesus.

This chapter elucidates Jesus' proclamation about the coming of God's reign and also about our grateful response to God's gift of our personal wholeness. After locating Jesus in his historical context, it describes our Lord from two perspectives. On the one hand, Jesus is the bearer of God's salvation; he is God's sacrament to us. In other words, Jesus is the human face of God. On the other hand, Jesus is our full, appreciative yes to God. He is our primary representative before God and thus the full realization of God's vision for us. These two approaches to the mystery of Jesus Christ lead to Jesus' view of his suffering, death, and resurrection and also to the post-Easter disciples' proclamation concerning the risen Christ.

I. Jesus in His Historical Context

Jesus was born in 4 BC or so and grew up in Nazareth. This village is located in Galilee, the Holy Land's northern hill country, which was also home to other prophetic figures from 100 BC to AD 100, figures such as Honi the Circle Drawer, John the Baptist, and Hanina ben Dosa. Each of these charismatic men set out to renew Israel's covenant with God but was ultimately repudiated in Jerusalem by the Jewish priests and the Roman authorities. In about AD 27, while likely working as a craftsman, Jesus was baptized in the Jordan River by John the Baptist. He began his public ministry after John was imprisoned by Herod Antipas, who, as a Roman official, dealt harshly with anyone or anything that jeopardized Rome's control of Palestine (Mark 1:14).

Jesus initially brought his message to people in the Galilean villages and occasionally went among the people in the neighboring regions. On the one hand, many people responded positively to Jesus, seeking him out even in remote areas. They were moved by his teachings, his cures, and his welcoming of them into his company. On the other hand, people did not know what to make of Jesus. He did not fit their diverse expectations (see chap. 5). He did not clearly resemble a new David (2 Sam 7:12), a new Aaron (Ps 110:4), a new Moses (Deut 18:18), a "son of man" coming on the clouds (Dan 7:13-14), or a good-shepherd leader (Zech 9:9-10). Moreover, he seemed destined to be a martyr as John the Baptist was.

The culminating point of Jesus' life occurred during his last days. According to the accounts of Mark, Matthew, and Luke, Jesus went to Jerusalem for the first and last time during his public ministry in about AD 30, just prior to Passover. As pilgrims gathered for Passover, he proclaimed his message near Jerusalem's temple, which was being renovated and enlarged from 19 BC to AD 63. Outraged by the market in the temple's courtyard, Jesus overturned some tables at which pilgrims bought animals and grains for sacrifice, criticizing the temple practices (Mark 11:12-25). On a Thursday, which was either the night before the start of Passover or the first night of Passover, Jesus held the "Last Supper" with his disciples. Afterward, he went to the Garden of Gethsemane in order to pray. When he was finished, he allowed himself to be seized by the temple police.

On Friday morning, the priests condemned Jesus to death for blasphemy, that is, for claiming to speak for God (Mark 15:1; see Deut 17:12; 18:20). Then they turned Jesus over to Pontius Pilate, the Roman prefect of Judea, who judged Jesus to be guilty of sedition against the Roman Empire. Pilate publicly declared this judgment in his mocking inscription on Jesus' cross: "The King of the Jews" (Mark 15:26). Jesus was immediately crucified and died before sundown on Friday. His crucifixion should have ended talk of Jesus as God's anointed one, for the book of Deuteronomy states that "anyone hung on a tree [i.e., crucified] is under God's curse" (Deut 21:23; Gal 3:13). How could the crucified Jesus be God's Messiah?

However, something happened. The women disciples who had watched Jesus' crucifixion, death, and burial on Friday returned to his tomb on Sunday. According to Jewish custom, they intended to anoint his body. But they found the tomb empty. According to Mark, they were met by "a young man, dressed in a white robe," who said to them: "Do not be alarmed; you are looking for Jesus of Nazareth, who was crucified. He has been raised; he is not here. . . . But go, tell his disciples and Peter that he is going ahead of you to Galilee; there you will see him, just as he told you" (Mark 16:6-7; cf. Matt 28:6; Luke 24:5; John 20:13-15).

Soon Jesus' followers, led by Peter, claimed that the crucified Jesus "was raised" by God from death and had "appeared" to them (1 Cor 15:3-5). Indeed, the crucified and risen Jesus had commissioned them to continue his mission and promised that he would come again with the fullness of God's kingdom. Forming their community, the church, the post-Easter disciples proclaimed the Good News about God's kingdom and our need for repentance and also about Jesus Christ as God's Son and the Savior of all people. As they undertook their mission, they awaited God's reign and the Lord Jesus' arrival or coming, his Parousia (Greek, *par*, "beside," + *ousia*, "being").

According to Christians, Jesus' life, death, and resurrection—the paschal mystery—was God's radical breakthrough in human history. However, according to the first century's Jewish priests and Roman officials, Jesus' death was simply one instance among many others of a false messiah who was severely punished for threatening the Holy Land's status quo, its *pax Romana*. Ironically, when the renovations of Jerusalem's temple were completed in AD 63, this completion prompted some Jews to revolt against Roman rule in AD 67. Three years later, the Roman general Titus suppressed the revolt and destroyed its catalyst, Jerusalem's temple. In doing so, he brought an end to the Sadducees, the priests responsible for Jesus' death.

II. Jesus' Message and Mission

As already noted, Jesus did not talk much about himself. Rather, he stressed God's offer of *salus*: "The time is fulfilled, and the kingdom of God has come near." Also, whereas self-proclaimed messiahs demand their followers' heteromony, Jesus called for theonomy: "Repent, and believe in the good news" (Mark 1:15). Let's consider both aspects of Jesus' Good News.

A. Jesus, Bearing God's Salvation

Jesus witnessed to the coming of "the kingdom of God." To put it another way, he proclaimed God's gift of *salus*, of God's "treasure hidden in a field" (Matt 13:44). In this perspective, as the bearer of God's love, Jesus can be likened to someone who is the public representative of his family and the family's business. To know this representative is to know the family and its business. Let's address four questions. Who is Jesus' God? What is God's kingdom or reign? When is this kingdom coming? Who is Jesus in relation to God?

1. Abba, Father

Jesus taught his followers to address God as Abba, Father: "Father, hallowed be your name. Your kingdom come. Give us each day our daily bread. And forgive us our sins, for we ourselves forgive everyone indebted to us. And do not bring us to the time of trial" (Luke 11:2-3; cf. Matt 6:9-13). In calling God "Abba," Jesus moved beyond God's usual names in the Old Testament as he sought to assist his listeners' understanding of the God whom Moses called YHWH (Exod 3:14-15; see chap 3). On one occasion, some Sadducees, that is, members of the temple's priestly families, came to Jesus and questioned him about his belief in God's resurrection of the dead, a belief that they rejected. However, Jesus declared that the Sadducees misunderstood the "book of Moses" (the book of Exodus) concerning "the story about the bush" in which Moses met "the God of Abraham, the God of Isaac, and the God of Jacob." They failed to grasp, Jesus said, that God "is God not of the dead, but of the living" (Mark 12:26-27). Abba, life's Source and Goal, will surely raise God's faithful people to eternal life after death.

Jesus told numerous parables concerning Abba. He said that God is similar to a shepherd who tirelessly seeks out the lost sheep (Matt 18:12-14), to a woman who cleans her entire house until she finds her lost coin (Luke 15:8-10), and to a merciful father who forgives his "prodigal" son (Luke 15:11-32). God reaches out to us even after we have turned our backs on God. God is Abba, to whom the psalmist prayed: "Show us your steadfast love, O LORD, and grant us your salvation. . . . Surely his salvation is at hand for those who fear him. . . . Steadfast love and faithfulness will meet; righteousness and peace will kiss each other. . . . The LORD will give what is good, and our land will yield its increase" (Ps 85:7-12).

2. God's Reign

Jesus' understanding of Abba was the wellspring from which flowed Jesus' words and deeds about God's kingdom. In his parable of the great banquet (Luke 14:15-24), Jesus recounts, "Someone gave a great dinner and invited many." But when it was time for the feast, the invited guests "began to make excuses" for their absence. When the host learned of their refusals, he immediately told his slave, "Go out at once into the streets and lanes of the town and bring in the poor, the crippled, the blind, and the lame." After doing this, the servant told the master, "There is still room" at the table. At this, the host charged the slave, "Go out into the roads and lanes, and compel people to come in, so that my house may be filled."

The parable's depiction of God shocked people. The host, God, gathers at the table the people whom Jesus' contemporaries saw as sinners. It was widely held that "the poor, the crippled, the blind, and the lame" were suffering because they or their parents had sinned (cf. John 9:2). However, God does not fit a theology of divine retribution (see chap. 4). God initially sends the slave to bring in people from "the town," hence, likely Jews. But the second time the host sends the messenger to bring in the people on "the roads and the lanes," hence, the people who were not Jewish or not practicing their Judaism. According to Jesus, God invites all people to enter God's kingdom. The God who called Abraham and Sarah to journey to Shechem (Gen 12), who charged Moses and the Hebrew slaves to make the exodus to the Holy Land (Exod 3), and who chose King David to be king (2 Sam 7) is the God who offers *salus* to all people.

Jesus witnessed to God's universal salvation not only by his words but also by his actions. He healed the daughter of the Syrophoenician woman (Mark 7:26) and also the Roman centurion's servant (Matt 8:13). Further, Jesus enacted the parable of the great dinner (Luke 14) whenever he ate with "sinners." On one occasion (Mark 6:30-44), Jesus and his disciples "had no leisure even to eat" because many people were seeking Jesus' help. Wanting to withdraw from the people, Jesus took his apostles in a boat across the Sea of Galilee. But the people followed him. When Jesus reached the shore, he "saw a great crowd; and he had compassion on them, because they were like sheep without a shepherd; and he began to teach them many things." In the late afternoon, the people were hungry, but there was no food to offer them in this "deserted place." Jesus instructed the disciples to have "all the people . . . sit down in groups on the grass" and to gather what food they could. The disciples gave Jesus "the five loaves and the two fish." Taking this food, Jesus "looked up to heaven, and blessed and broke the loaves, and gave them to his disciples to set before the people; and he divided the two fish among them all." Amazingly, there was plenty of food. "And all ate and were filled; and they took up twelve baskets full of broken pieces [of bread] and of the fish."

In this meal, Jesus dramatized the parable of the great feast. As the host, Jesus offered the people an experience of God's *salus*, the kingdom. Having "compassion" on the people, Jesus invited them—as individuals and as a community—into Abba's love. In order to show that God invisibly nurtures us, Jesus replicated God's feeding of manna to the Israelites in the desert (Exod 16:1-18; cf. 2 Kgs 4:42-44). Even though the "great crowd" likely included both Jews and non-Jews, Jesus did not differentiate among them. He welcomed everyone to his "great dinner," at which people sat side by side with strangers and "sinners." Jesus' miracle involved both his multiplying of the "five loaves and the two fish" and also his opening of people's hearts, minds, and wills to sharing their meal with strangers and "sinners." In sum, Jesus gave the people a taste of God's great banquet, the kingdom, to which "I have come to call not the righteous but sinners" (Mark 2:17).

Jesus also proclaimed God's reign as he treated each person as God's "treasure," a "pearl of great value" (Matt 13:44-45). For example, Jesus warmly greeted the tax collector Zacchaeus and even dined at his home (Luke 19:1-10). Also, he cherished each child: "Whoever welcomes one such child in my name welcomes me" (Mark 9:37).

In particular, Jesus showed God's love as he related to women. In ancient Israelite society, women had no legal or religious rights; they were regarded as the property of their fathers or husbands. But Jesus respected women as human persons. Once, as he was entering the village of Nain, he noticed the funeral procession for a widow's "only son." Without her son and without her husband, this woman likely faced dire poverty. Jesus immediately "had compassion for her." Breaking social convention, he approached the widow and said, "Do not weep." Turning to the dead son, Jesus declared, "Young man, I say to you, rise!" So it happened. "The dead man sat up and began to speak" (Luke 7:11-17).

Jesus performed miracles in order to call attention not to himself but to the character of Abba and of Abba's new creation. He foreshadowed the fullness of *salus* among us when he exorcized a man of his demon (Mark 1:21-28), forgave the sins of a paralyzed man and also healed him (2:1-12), and calmed a storm on the Sea of Galilee (4:35-41). Further, he symbolically foreshadowed God's resurrection of the dead when he resuscitated the widow of Nain's son (Luke 7), the daughter of Jairus (Mark 5:42), and Lazarus (John 11:44).

In his words, deeds, and relating to people, Jesus declared that Abba offers us *salus*, personal wholeness in union with God and in communion with one another and the earth. In response to John the Baptist's question whether Jesus was God's anointed one, Jesus told John's disciples, "Go and tell John what you hear and see: the blind receive their sight, the lame walk, the lepers are cleansed, the deaf hear, the dead are raised, and the poor have the good news brought to them" (Matt 11:4-6). With these words, Jesus was alluding to Isaiah's words concerning the arrival of the LORD's Messiah with the in-breaking of God's new creation (Isa 61:1-3).

3. The Coming of God's Kingdom

Jesus took seriously Israel's expectation that God would soon "create new heavens and a new earth" (Isa 65:17; see chap. 5). Zephaniah had declared, "The great day of the Lord is near, . . . a day of wrath" (1:14-15). Expecting this "day," Joel had urged his listeners to "return to the LORD, your God, for he is gracious and merciful" (2:13). These expressions of prophetic eschatology were complemented by the apocalyptic view of God's judgment against Satan and Satan's "beasts," the world empires. According to the book of Daniel, the "Ancient One" would put the "beast" to death, and he would confer on the "son of man" complete authority so that "all peoples, nations, and languages should serve him" (7:9-14). These prophetic and apocalyptic themes were known to Jesus, who wove them together in his message concerning God's coming reign.

While Jesus lessened prophetic eschatology's emphasis on divine wrath, he promoted its theme that God is at work in history. On the one hand, Jesus stressed the "already." He compared the in-breaking of God's kingdom to the growth of a mustard seed. This seed is "the smallest of all seeds," and it grows so slowly that its development is almost imperceptible. Nevertheless, it "becomes the greatest of all shrubs" (Mark 4:32). So it is with God's salvation. On the other hand, Jesus stressed the "not yet." He told the parable of the vineyard whose self-serving tenants claimed ownership of the vineyard, abused the true owner's messengers, and killed his son. "What then will the owner of the vineyard do? He will come and destroy the tenants and give the vineyard to others" (12:9). So too will God renew God's vineyard in truth and love.

At the same time, Jesus acknowledged that evil is at work in the world; thus, he conveyed an apocalyptic eschatology. In the wilderness, he successfully struggled with Satan (Mark 1:13), and in his ministry he repeatedly exorcized people's demons (e.g., 1:23-26). When he was accused of collaborating with Satan, also known as Beelzebul, he responded, "How can Satan cast out Satan?" After explaining that he acted with God's power, Jesus added that his mission included "tying up the strong man," that is, binding the bully Satan once and for all (3:22-27). Jesus even spoke of a cosmic showdown when "nation will rise against nation, and kingdom against kingdom." Then the Son of Man will appear "with great power and glory," and he "will send out the angels, and gather his elect from the four winds, from the ends of the earth to the ends of heaven" (13:26-27). Although Jesus did not know the day of God's final judgment, he urged readiness for its arrival: "Beware, keep alert; for you do not know when the time will come" (13:32-33).

4. Lord Jesus, God's Son

Jesus implicitly communicated his sense of himself as God's Son. Drawing on his exceptional intimacy with Abba, he taught his followers to pray the "Lord's Prayer," the "Our Father" (Matt 6:9-13; Luke 11:2-3). When he neared his final confrontation with his opponents, he prayed in the Garden of Gethsemane, "Abba, Father, for you all things are possible; remove this cup from me; yet, not what I want, but what you want" (Mark 14:36). While teaching us to trust Abba, Jesus differentiated between our relationship with God and Jesus' unique filial bond with God. He expressed this difference when he taught, "All things have been handed over to me by my Father; and no one knows the Son except the Father, and no one knows the Father except the Son and anyone to whom the Son chooses to reveal him" (11:27). In other words, Jesus held that our relating to Abba occurs in union with Jesus' relating to Abba.

Jesus' awareness of his singular relationship with God manifested itself in his extraordinary personal authority. Jesus' contemporaries held that God alone can forgive sins. In light of this belief, John the Baptist offered not the forgiveness of sins but "a baptism of repentance for the forgiveness of sins [by God]" (Mark 1:4). However, Jesus claimed to forgive sins. To the paralyzed man he said, "Son, your sins are forgiven." The religious leaders immediately grasped the implication: "Why does this fellow speak in this way? It is blasphemy! Who can forgive sins but God alone?" (Mark 2:5-7; cf. Luke 7:36-50). Either Jesus was (and is) God's Son or he deserved death for his blasphemy.

Further, Jesus spoke of himself as the bridegroom celebrating among the wedding guests who would fast after he "is taken away from them" (Mark 2:20). He went so far as to say that he would assign his disciples their seats at God's great feast: "You are those who have stood by me in my trials; and I confer on you, just as my Father has conferred on me, a kingdom, so that you may eat and drink at my table in my kingdom, and you will sit on thrones judging the twelve tribes of Israel" (Luke 22:28-30).

After Easter, Christians recalled how Jesus' words and deeds implied his singular filial bond with God, and they explicitly identified Jesus as God's Son. St. Paul held that Jesus Christ is the "Son of God with power according to the spirit of holiness by resurrection from the dead" (Rom 1:4). St. John declared, "Jesus is the Messiah, the Son of God" (John 20:31).

B. Jesus, Saying Our Yes to God

Along with proclaiming God's offer of salvation, Jesus taught his listeners how to welcome this ultimate reality into their lives: "Repent, and believe in the good news" (Mark 1:15). As we considered in chapter 2, human beings are born with a dark urge to try to be "like God" (Gen 3:5). With Adam and Eve, we are attracted to radical heteronomy and to radical autonomy. However, we are called by God to theonomy. Jesus lived in radical faithfulness to Abba; he lived out the right relationship with God in which we're meant to live. In this, he gave our grateful, total acceptance of God's *salus*. In this perspective, Jesus is similar to a soccer team's captain who has ties with every player, inspires the team to play its best, and represents the team to the head coach, the referees, and the general public. In this perspective, let's explore Jesus' teachings on *metanoia*, on theonomy, on living with hope, and on Jesus as the Son of Man.

1. Personal Transformation

Jesus made it clear: our appropriate response to God's salvation is personal transformation, repentance. During the exodus Moses and the Israelites responded to God's deliverance with their conversion at the

Red Sea and with their subsequent adoption of the Ten Commandments (Exod 14; 20; see chap. 3). Challenged by the prophet Nathan, King David repented of his seduction of Bathsheba, undergoing a radical change of heart and mind (2 Sam 12:13). Centuries later, John the Baptist had called for "a baptism of repentance for the forgiveness of sins" (Mark 1:4). In receiving John's baptism, Jesus manifested his solidarity with us. Being one with us, he taught, "Repent, for the kingdom of heaven has come near" (Matt 4:17).

A personal transformation is not easy. It may happen with the admission of a specific act of wrongdoing, as occurred after St. Peter denied knowing Jesus (Mark 14:72). Or it may occur as someone renounces his preoccupation with himself and accepts himself as God's treasure. Such is the story of the Samaritan woman's encounter with Jesus at Jacob's well (John 4:1-42). Although *metanoia* assumes various forms, it entails the decentering of our egos and our recentering in God. In particular, it involves our relinquishing of our false selves, our searching for our true center, and our eventually finding God and our true selves as God intends us (see chap. 3).

Jesus referred to this process in his parables of the treasure and the pearl, which include words (in italics below) that imply loss, active waiting, and discovery. Jesus said, "Again, the kingdom of heaven is like a treasure hidden in a field, which someone *found* and *hid*; then in his joy he goes and *sells all* that he has and *buys* that field." He also taught, "Again, the kingdom of heaven is like a merchant in *search* of fine pearls; on *finding* one pearl of great value, he went and *sold all* that he had and *bought* it" (Matt 13:44-45; italics added).

Jesus compared a person's *metanoia* to a death and resurrection: "For those who want to save their life will lose it, and those who lose their life for my sake, and for the sake of the gospel, will save it" (Mark 8:35). Indeed, a person's reorientation is similar to what a seed goes through to become fruitful: "Very truly, I tell you, unless a grain of wheat falls into the earth and dies, it remains just a single grain; but if it dies, it bears much fruit. Those who love their life lose it, and those who hate their life in this world will keep it for eternal life" (John 12:24-25).

2. A New Way of Life

Since a personal transformation does not happen all at once, Jesus called for an entirely new form of life: theonomy. A person's *metanoia* develops into a form of life in which, in gratitude for God's *salus*, the person lives according to the two great commandments: love of God and love of neighbor. On one occasion, a Jewish scribe asked Jesus, "Which commandment is the first of all?" (Mark 12:28-34). Jesus said that the first is the *Shema* (Deut 6:4-5), which restates the first of the Ten Commandments (Exod 20:2-3): "Hear, O Israel: the Lord our God, the Lord is one; you shall love the Lord your God with all your heart, and with all your soul, and with all your mind, and with all your strength." Jesus immediately added that the second most important commandment is Leviticus 19:18, "You shall love your neighbor as yourself." The scribe agreed with Jesus and added that obeying the two great commandments "is much more important than all whole burnt offerings and sacrifices." Seeing that the scribe "answered wisely," Jesus replied, "You are not far from the kingdom of God."

Jesus singled out the two great "laws" in order to stress that our yes to God's *salus* involves much more than outward conformity to the Ten Commandments and other religious and moral prescriptions. Rather, our acceptance of God's gift should engage our whole selves. This is not surprising. Two people who love one another exceed the "rules" as they communicate with each other and care for each other. Parents far surpass the limits of their previous generosity as they make sacrifices for their children. So too as we respond to God's grace and abide by the Ten Commandments and the church's norms, we are guided and inspired by the Spirit to go beyond these laws as we are faithful to God and attend to other people's needs. Living the essence or spirit of the laws, we are lifted up like a kite away from the entangling branches of selfishness, self-denigration, and narcissism, and we are borne by the Spirit into authentic love of God, self, neighbor, and the earth.

Jesus praised people who orient their hearts, minds, and wills to God and their neighbor. He acknowledged their theonomy in his Beatitudes (blessings): "Blessed are the poor in spirit. . . . Blessed are those who mourn. . . . Blessed are the meek. . . . Blessed are those who hunger and thirst for righteousness. . . . Blessed are the merciful. . . . Blessed are the pure in heart. . . . Blessed are the peacemakers" (Matt 5:3-10; cf. Luke 6:17-38).

Finally, Jesus rejected the law of retaliation, the *lex talionis*: "You shall give life for life, eye for eye, tooth for tooth, hand for hand, foot for foot, burn for burn, wound for wound, stripe for stripe" (Exod 21:23-24). Jesus declared, "You have heard that it was said, 'An eye for an eye and a tooth for a tooth.' But I say to you, Do not resist an evildoer. But if anyone strikes you on the right cheek, turn the other also" (Matt 5:38-39). Why did Jesus reject the *lex talionis?* Retaliation harms our hearts, our minds, and our wills. It disrupts our movement toward personal wholeness, for it impels us to do things that distance us from our consciences. In contrast, Jesus stressed the Golden Rule: "In everything do to others as you would have them do to you" (Matt 7:12). Yet even following the Golden Rule does not suffice. According to Jesus, we must "love one another as I have loved you. No one has greater love than this, to lay down one's life for one's friends" (John 15:12-13).

3. Living with Hope

During his ministry, Jesus taught his followers to hope in God, that is, to anticipate that God is already seeking what's best for us and that God will ultimately bring us to the fullness of life in God's kingdom. In other words, he affirmed God's rhetorical question to Abraham and Sarah: "Is anything too wonderful for the LORD?" (Gen 17:14).

Jesus taught us to pray the Lord's Prayer with its words of hope: "Father, . . . Your kingdom come. Give us each day our daily bread. And forgive us our sins. . . . And do not bring us to the time of trial" (Luke 11:2-4). Praying for God's guidance and strength, Jesus lived in anticipation of God's bringing Jesus himself and all of God's people beyond life's obstacles and dead ends to the fullness of salvation. This anticipation, this hope, manifested itself in Jesus' prayer for God's guidance and strength during his temptations (Mark 1:12), during the numerous times when he prayed in a "deserted place" (1:35; cf. 6:46), during his decision making in the Garden of Gethsemane (14:32-42), and during his dying on the cross (15:34).

Moreover, hope directed Jesus to look for God's presence in the lives of the people with whom he interacted. When he detected the in-breaking of God's *salus*, he nurtured this love. Consider how he reached out to a leper (Mark 1:40-45), to the hemorrhaging woman (5:21-34), and to the blind Bartimaeus (10:46). Jesus did not despair when he saw weeds growing up among the wheat. Rather, he nurtured the wheat while tolerating the weeds. Encouraging us to do the same, he advised, "Let them both grow together until the harvest" (Matt 13:30). Even though Jesus met continual resistance, he remained hopeful that God's reign, "like yeast," remains active in people's lives, the "three measures of flour" (13:33).

Hope also enabled Jesus to expect the future fullness of God's kingdom as he endured the limitations and frustrations of dealing with his opponents. He urged us to learn from the five bridesmaids "who took flasks of oil with their lamps" when they "went to meet the bridegroom." As a result, unlike the five "foolish" bridesmaids who had not brought oil, the five "wise" bridesmaids were ready when the bridegroom came and "went with him into the wedding banquet" (Matt 25:1-13).

During his last days, Jesus foresaw the full arrival of God's reign among human beings. At the Last Supper, he assured his disciples, "Amen, I say to you, I shall not drink again the fruit of the vine until the day when I drink it new in the kingdom of God" (Mark 14:15). With these words, Jesus was alluding to Isaiah's hopeful vision of God's banquet in the new creation: "On this mountain the LORD of hosts will make for all peoples a feast of rich food, a feast of well-aged wines. . . . [God] will swallow up death forever. Then the Lord GOD will wipe away the tears from all faces. . . . This is the LORD for whom we have waited; let us be glad and rejoice in his salvation" (Isa 25:6-10; cf. Rev 19:6).

4. Jesus, the Son of Man

In calling for our *metanoia*, Jesus stood (and still stands) with all people who yearn for salvation. In particular, he identified with villagers and bound himself to the poor, the marginalized, and the shunned. He summoned his twelve apostles from the ordinary people and drew into his company women who, simply because of their gender, were disregarded by the religious and civil officials. Moreover, in order to express his solidarity with people, he spoke of himself as the "Son of Man." He adopted this title from Psalm 8:4, Ezekiel 2:1, and Daniel 7:13, where it functions in the sense of "a mortal," "a man in union with all people," and "a servant of human beings." Simultaneously, Jesus tailored the title's meaning to himself as he used it in three distinct, though interrelated, ways.

First, Jesus applied "Son of Man" to himself as the herald of God's kingdom. For example, after he dined with Zacchaeus and initiated this tax collector's conversion, he said, "Today salvation has come to this house because he too is a son of Abraham. For the Son of Man came to seek out and to save the lost" (Mark 2:28).

Second, Jesus used the title in relation to himself as God's martyr-Messiah who would remain faithful to his God-given mission, even at the cost of his life. He voiced his commitment in these words or in ones similar to them: "The Son of Man is to be betrayed into human hands, and they will kill him, and three days after being killed, he will rise again" (Mark 9:31).

Third, Jesus referred to himself as the "Son of Man" who would oversee God's final judgment of all people. He taught, "Those who are ashamed of me and of my words in this adulterous and sinful genera-tion, of them the Son of Man will also be ashamed when he comes in the glory of his Father with the holy angels" (Mark 8:38).

In sum, Jesus, the Son of Man, is one with us as we receive the in-breaking of God's salvation. He heals, teaches, and encourages us. He abides with us as we suffer, die, and move toward new life. Finally, at the Last Judgment, he will embrace us and usher us into God's heavenly banquet. In these three ways, he invites us to share in his unambiguous yes to God's gift of our personal wholeness in relation to God, ourselves, one another, and creation.

III. Jesus' View of His Death and Resurrection

Jesus—God's Son and the Son of Man—dedicated his life to his proclamation: "The time is fulfilled, and the kingdom of God has come near; repent, and believe in the good news" (Mark 1:15). But how did Jesus perceive his suffering, death, and resurrection?

A. Jesus' View of His Death

Jesus saw his passion and death not as his life's goal but as the means by which he would ultimately secure God's reign in creation and his-tory. As a mother endures her labor pains for the sake of her baby, Jesus submitted to his suffering and death for the sake of our *salus*. In this regard, Jesus employed various metaphors and images when he spoke about his fate in Jerusalem. Consider these five motifs.

1. Jesus identified himself as a prophet such as Elijah, Jeremiah, and John the Baptist. Referring to himself, he said, "Truly I tell you, no prophet is accepted in the prophet's hometown" (Luke 4:24; cf. Mark 6:4), and "Jerusalem, Jerusalem, the city that kills the prophets and stones those who are sent to it" (Matt 23:37).

2. Jesus likened himself to a martyr like the priest Eleazar, who intended his death as an act of atonement or reconciliation (4 Macc 6:28-29). At the Last Supper, Jesus said that his "body [is] for you" (1 Cor 11:24) and that his "blood [is] poured out for many" (Mark 14:24; cf. Exod 24:8). Jesus may have also seen his life in relation to Isaiah's fourth Servant Song (Isa 52:13–53:12; cf. Acts 8:26-35). In particular, he may have had this Servant Song in mind when he told James and John, "The cup that I drink you will drink; and with the baptism with which I am baptized, you will be baptized" (Mark 10:39).

3. Jesus called his life a "ransom" from Satan (Mark 10:45); he spoke of his "tying up the strong man," Satan, so that he could "plunder his property" (3:27). In this vein, he freed people from the demons (e.g., the addictions) that controlled them (1:23-26; 5:13; 9:14-29).

4. Jesus linked his death with God's self-sacrificing love. He saw it as God's gift of salvation. In all that he did, Jesus lived for others. He explained that he must leave one village and go to another so that "I may proclaim the message there also; for that is what I came to do" (Mark 1:38). He denied himself food, drink, and rest for the sake of his mission (6:34). In everything, he enacted God's search for God's lost sheep (Matt 18:12-14). As the shepherd-leader, he entered Jerusalem riding a colt and laid down his life for the sheep's well-being (Mark 11:7; John 10; cf. Zech 9:9; 13:7). He held that he was giving his life to renew God's covenant with God's people (Mark 14:24; cf. Exod 24:4-8).

5. Jesus died because of his faithfulness to God, Abba, and to the coming of God's reign. He connected his suffering and death with his yes on our behalf to the Father's offer of salvation to all people. At the start of his ministry, he rejected Satan's temptations (Mark 1:13), and, as he neared his mission's end, he reaffirmed his fidelity to the Father: "Abba, Father, for you all things are possible; remove this cup from me; yet, not what I want, but what you want" (14:36). Jesus, the Son of Man, lived unto death his teaching that "those who lose their life . . . for the sake of the gospel will save it" (8:35).

Jesus used these diverse images and motifs in order to impart his view that his suffering and death were congruent with his mission, indeed essential to it. However, in employing these various figures of speech, he did not give a theory or explanation of why he would suffer and die on the cross. Further, he never said or even suggested that the Father required or desired Jesus' crucifixion. In other words, he did not view his death as propitiating or appeasing God. Jesus attributed his crucifixion to his human enemies and to Satan, not to God. While he freed us from Satan, he saw no need to ransom us from Abba, life's Source and Goal.

B. Jesus' View of His Resurrection

Jesus also anticipated that his mission included his resurrection. He believed that his life would conclude not in a catastrophe but in a victory, in what Tolkien called a "eucatastrophe," a happy ending (see chap. 5). Moreover, Jesus believed that his victory would not only vindicate him but also have saving or salvific significance for all people, that his life, death, and resurrection would deliver all people from evil, death, and meaninglessness into eternal life.

In his response to the Sadducees, Jesus affirmed his belief in God's resurrection of the dead, declaring that God "is God not of the dead, but of the living" (Mark 12:27). He surely knew too Daniel's affirmation that "many of those who sleep in the dust of the earth shall awake. . . . Those who are wise shall shine like the brightness of the sky, and those who lead many to righteousness, like the stars forever and ever" (Dan 12:2-3). Further, Jesus knew the belief in God's resurrection held by Jewish martyrs: "One cannot but choose to die at the hands of mortals and to cherish the hope God gives of being raised again by him" (2 Macc 7:14).

At the Last Supper, Jesus clarified his belief in his resurrection. He and his disciples ate the bread that he identified as "my body" and drank the cup's wine that he identified as "my blood of the covenant, which is poured out for many." Then he declared, "Truly I tell you, I will never again drink of the fruit of the vine until that day when I drink it new in the kingdom of God" (Mark 14:22-25). With these words, Jesus communicated his vision of being raised from the dead and being reunited with his disciples in the last age at God's eternal banquet.

A dying person's words are often self-revealing. Sometimes they sum up someone's orientation throughout his or her life. This is true of Jesus' last words. As he was dying on the cross, Jesus prayed aloud—according to Mark, Matthew, and Luke—Psalm 22:1a, "My God, my God, why have you forsaken me?" (Mark 15:34). These are words of abandonment, of distance from God. They are not, however, the end of the story. Rather, they commence the psalmist's lamentation that moves from darkness into light (see chap. 4).

Psalm 22:1b begins with a complaint: "Why are you [God] so far from helping me, from the words of my groaning?" This question generates the petition, "Do not be far from me" (Ps 22:11) and "But you, O LORD, do not be far away" (22:19). This petition brings about the shift to acknowledging God's presence amid absurd suffering: "From the horns of the wild oxen you have rescued me. I will tell our name to my brothers and sisters. . . . You who fear the LORD, praise him!" Next, the acknowledgment of God's presence prompts the declaration that God "heard when I cried to him" (22:24b). There follows a testimony of hope: "Those who seek him shall praise the LORD. May your hearts live forever!" (22:26b). Further: "To him, indeed, shall all who sleep in the earth bow down; . . . and I shall live for him" (22:29). Having begun in the "Pit," Psalm 22 culminates at the threshold of eternal life: "Future generations will . . . proclaim his deliverance to a people yet unborn, saying that he has done it" (22:31). In sum, Jesus' dying words manifest his hope that God would "raise" him beyond death, chaos, and Satan's grasp to a radically new life in eternal union with God.

IV. The Church's Message and Mission

"Peace be with you" were the first words that the crucified and risen Jesus declared to his apostles (Luke 24:36; John 20:19, 21, 26). This post-Easter greeting reaffirms Jesus' eternal solidarity with his followers. Further, it announces that God's "new heavens and a new earth" have commenced in Jesus, God's anointed one (Isa 65:17; 2 Pet 3:13; Rev 21:1). Jesus is the "firstborn" of God's people in the last age (Rom 8:29; Col 1:15, 18).

Jesus' disciples were not, however, looking for him; they were not even awaiting his return. All of them, except for a few women, had fled. They had gone into hiding out of "fear" (John 20:19). Months earlier on the Sea of Galilee, they had been "afraid" in the squall (Mark 4:40) and "were filled with great awe" when the squall immediately abated after Jesus said to the sea, "Peace! Be still!" (Mark 4:39). After Jesus' death, they were even more awestruck when Jesus "appeared" to them. To calm them, he said, "Greetings! . . . Do not be afraid" (Matt 28:10). No one anticipated that the LORD would do something so wonderful as to raise Jesus to eternal life ahead of all of God's people. But in his resurrection appearances, Jesus Christ gave the definitive answer to the question, "Is anything too wonderful for the LORD?" (Gen 18:14).

While Jesus' followers did not witness his resurrection, they saw his empty tomb, were met by Jesus in his appearances, and were enlightened and inspired by the Holy Spirit about Jesus' new life in God. Given these three elements, the apostles and disciples were transformed. They proclaimed through their words, their actions, and their persons, "This Jesus God raised up, and of that all of us are witnesses" (Acts 2:32). When Jesus had been arrested, Peter had denied even knowing Jesus. But in response to Jesus' resurrection appearances, Peter manifested extraordinary courage as he reassembled Jesus' followers, publicly preached about the Lord Jesus, and performed miracles in Jesus' name (2:14-36). Although the Pharisee Saul had persecuted Jesus' followers, he underwent a conversion in response to his encounter with the risen Christ. He became Paul, God's messenger "to the Gentiles" (Rom 15:9). Moreover, although women were expected to remain hidden within their homes, Jesus' women followers such as Phoebe, Prisca, Mary, and Junia became public leaders in their Christian communities (16:1-6). Such was the impact upon the disciples of the Lord Jesus' appearances and words: "Peace be with you," and "Do not be afraid."

As stated earlier, Jesus' post-Easter followers enlarged the Good News or Gospel that Jesus had explicitly taught. Although Jesus—unlike today's self-appointed messiahs—did not say much about himself, Jesus' disciples proclaimed Jesus as "the Messiah" (Mark 8:29). To be more precise, they announced "that Jesus is the Christ, the Son of God," and "that through believing you may have life in his name" (John 20:31). According to St. Paul, Jesus Christ is God's Son, "who was descended from David according to the flesh and was declared to be Son of God with power according to the spirit of holiness by resurrection from the dead" (Rom 1:1-4). This truth concerning Jesus' unique identity as God's Son stands side by side with the truth concerning Jesus' singular role as God's Savior of all people. Paul "handed on" this Good News when he taught that "Christ died for our sins in accordance with the scriptures, and that he was buried, and that he was raised on the third day in accordance with the scriptures, and that he appeared to Cephas, then to the twelve" (1 Cor 15:3-5). After meeting Jesus through the initiative of the Samaritan woman, the villagers confessed that "this is truly the Savior of the world" (John 4:42).

These two truths about Jesus Christ have vast implications. One is that all people—in union with Jesus Christ through the Spirit—may now share in God's resurrection of the dead and participate in God's eternal life. St. Paul assured the Christians at Thessalonica in AD 49: "For the Lord himself, with a cry of command . . . will descend from heaven, and the dead in Christ will rise first. Then we who are alive . . . will be caught up in the clouds together with them to meet the Lord in the air, and so we will be with the Lord forever" (1 Thess 4:16-17).

A second implication is that Jesus Christ through the Holy Spirit continues to be present to God's people. According to St. Matthew, Jesus' last words to his disciples were "And remember, I am with you always, to the end of the age" (Matt 28:20). Reflecting on Christ's presence to us, the theologian Karl Rahner has observed: "It is really possible to love Jesus, across all space and time. . . . We read Holy Scripture in the way two lovers gaze at one another in the living of their daily life together. . . . We allow ourselves really to be told something by him that otherwise we should not have known for our life."[1]

The implications of Jesus' life, death, and resurrection—that is, of the paschal mystery—were not lost upon the first Christians. Soon after Easter they realized that henceforth personal knowledge of Jesus Christ would require our knowing a person who not only lived in the past but who also abides in the present and will come again in God's last age. Indeed, Jesus Christ has fractured our conceptual framework of time and space in a way only he could bring about. This belief that Jesus Christ, God's Son and Savior for all people, is still present to God's people generated the gospels of Mark, Matthew, Luke, and John and also inspired the book of Revelation. To these writings we turn in chapter 7 and chapter 8.

Chapter 7

Gospel Portraits of Jesus Christ

While walking with his followers to Caesarea Philippi's villages, Jesus asked, "Who do people say that I am?" The disciples gave various answers: "John the Baptist," "Elijah," and "one of the prophets." Then Jesus asked, "But who do you say that I am?" Peter answered, "You are the Messiah." Affirming Peter's response, Jesus "sternly ordered them not to tell anyone about him." He also clarified the meaning of "Messiah," "Christ," as ascribed to him: "The Son of Man must undergo great suffering, and be rejected by the elders, the chief priests, and the scribes, and be killed, and after three days rise again" (Mark 8:27-31).

This dialogue between the Lord and his followers is still happening. Today the crucified and risen Jesus in the Spirit often asks us, "But who do you say that I am?" The question of Jesus' personal identity is posed anew for every Christian because it has no single, completely satisfactory answer. It directs us to Jesus Christ, whom we can increasingly know and love but never fully grasp. Each answer leaves much left unsaid about the Lord. For this reason, the church identifies Jesus Christ by means of the four canonical gospels, by numerous biblical titles and biblical texts, and by church teachings such as the Nicene Creed (AD 325 and 381) and the doctrine of Chalcedon (AD 451). The gospel portraits are the subject of this chapter.

While the gospels of Mark, Matthew, Luke, and John agree that Jesus is the Christ, God's Son and the Savior of all people, they give differing depictions of the Lord Jesus. According to Mark, Jesus Christ is the martyr-Messiah. According to Matthew, he is the teacher-Messiah. According to Luke, the Lord Jesus is God's envoy-Messiah, and according

121

to John, he is the good-shepherd–Messiah. Let's examine these biblical portraits and then reflect on Jesus Christ as "our Savior," the key to our personal identities (Titus 3:6).

I. St. Mark on the Martyr-Messiah

Writing in about AD 70 to his persecuted Christian community, the evangelist Mark depicts Jesus as God's anointed one who accepted suffering and death so that the arrival of God's kingdom might be secured in creation and history. In this view, the crucified and risen Jesus Christ now offers hope to all people who are themselves undergoing hardships.

A. Jesus Christ, Winning by Losing

In order to access Mark's gospel, consider the common experience of fighting an illness. Who among us has not come down with the flu when working on a project, preparing for the holidays, or caring for other people? We often resist the illness until we have fulfilled our responsibilities, and then we let it crash down on us like a massive wave. Falling into bed, we anticipate that the illness will run its course and then lose its power over us so that our health will return.

According to Mark, Jesus initially declared his message and resisted his opponents, including Satan (Mark 1:12-13). But he eventually gave in to his enemies (8:27-31), trusting that they would lose their power over him as the Father brought him beyond death to new life. This is what happened. After dying on a cross on a Friday, he was buried. But on Sunday, three of Jesus' women disciples found his tomb empty and were told by "a young man" that "he has been raised; he is not here. . . . He is going ahead of you to Galilee" (16:6-7). Jesus had died with hope in God. As he said, he came among us "to give his life as a ransom for many" (10:45). How has Mark formed this portrait?

B. Mark's Literary Elements

The student editors of a high school yearbook receive from other students the photographs of the school's activities and events as well as the data about its wins and losses in its academic and athletic competitions. After these materials are amassed, they assemble everything in relation to this year's theme—for example, "Standing Out" or "Making a Difference." In a similar way, Mark received materials from Christian oral traditions and edited them in order to depict Jesus Christ as the martyr-Messiah. This can be seen in Mark's literary design, his use of titles for Jesus, and the way in which he crafted the passion narrative— that is, the story of Jesus' suffering, death, and resurrection.

First, Mark has structured his account into two major parts united by a pivotal scene. In the gospel's first half (Mark 1:14–8:26), Jesus pursues his mission with authority and power. For example, he stills a squall on the Sea of Galilee (4:35-41). He also casts out people's "unclean spirits." As he does so, they cry out, "I know who you are, the Holy One of God" (1:25), and "You are the Son of God" (3:11). Jesus is the powerful Son of God. At the gospel's turning point, Peter confesses, "You are the Messiah" (8:29). In the gospel's second half (8:31–15:47), Jesus deliberately relinquishes his power. As in the parable of the vineyard (12:1-12), Jesus, the son of the vineyard's owner, permits the wicked tenants to seize him and kill him. Why? After this apparent tragedy, the owner "will come and destroy the tenants and give the vineyard to others" (12:9). In Jesus' resurrection, God has conquered the wicked tenants, namely, evil, meaninglessness, and death. At this good news, Jesus' followers are overcome with "terror and amazement" (16:8).

Second, Mark identifies Jesus by means of the titles "Son of God" and "Son of Man." At the outset, he writes, "The beginning of the good news of Jesus Christ, the Son of God" (Mark 1:1). He subsequently notes that Jesus is called "Son of God" or its equivalents by the demons (1:24; 3:11; 5:7), the high priest (14:61), and the Roman centurion at Jesus' cross (15:39), as well as by God at Jesus' baptism and transfiguration (1:11; 9:7). Mark simultaneously recounts that Jesus applied "Son of Man" to himself regarding his ministry (2:18), his suffering, death, and resurrection (8:31), and his coming at the Last Judgment (13:26). Moreover, the evangelist arranges the material from the oral traditions so that Jesus tells his disciples three times in close proximity that he, the Son of Man, will be put to death and raised to life (8:31; 9:31; 10:33). By means of this repetition, Mark links the crucified Jesus with the title "Son of Man." Yet, as already noted, Mark tells that the centurion stood before the crucified Jesus and said, "Truly this man was God's Son!" (15:39). In sum, the two views of Jesus as God's Son and as the Son of Man come together at the cross: Jesus Christ, the Son of God and the Son of Man, is the martyr-Messiah.

Third, Mark recounts Jesus' suffering, death, and resurrection (Mark 15:1–16:6) in light of the book of Isaiah's fourth Servant Song (Isa 52:13–53:12). (The added italics below show the textual similarities.) Isaiah's "Suffering Servant" is an individual or community that dedicates its misery at the hands of abusers for the removal of sins' effects and thus for reconciliation, atonement (see chap. 4). The fourth Servant Song begins with an anticipation of its outcome: "See, my *servant* shall prosper; he shall *be exalted and lifted up* (52:13). Then it recalls that this servant "*was despised and rejected by others; a man of suffering*" (53:3). He "*was oppressed . . . yet he did not open his mouth*; like a lamb *led to the slaughter . . .* so that he *did not open his mouth*" (53:7). He was "*cut off from the land of the living*" (53:8). "They made his grave with *the wicked* and his *tomb* with the rich, . . . and there was *no deceit in his mouth*" (53:9). But the servant will be victorious. "Out of his anguish he *shall see light*" (53:11). In the end God declares, "I will allot him a portion with the great" (53:12).

Now, observe how the fourth Servant Song has influenced the language and imagery of Mark's passion narrative. After condemning Jesus to death on Friday morning, the priests "*bound Jesus, led him away, and handed him over to Pilate*" (Mark 15:1). Pilate questioned Jesus, who answered Pilate's first question but then "*made no further reply*" (15:5). Pilate deliberated, had Jesus flogged, and then "*handed him over to be crucified*" (15:15). The soldiers "*led him* into the courtyard of the palace," where they mocked him (15:16). Finally, they "*led him out to crucify him*" (15:20), and they executed Jesus along with "*two bandits*" (15:28). As people walked by, they "*derided*" Jesus (15:29); the chief priests "*were also mocking him*" (15:31). After Jesus' death, Joseph laid his body "in a *tomb*" (15:46). On Sunday, the women returned to the tomb, found it empty, and learned that "*he has been raised; he is not here*" (16:6).

Mark's passion narrative is the story of God's Suffering Servant, Jesus, who has made "his life a ransom for many" (Mark 10:45). Adding to this depiction is Mark's two-part narrative of Jesus possessing authority and power as God's Son and then choosing to relinquish them (8:27-31), becoming vulnerable as the Son of Man. Yet on the cross Jesus shows that he is the Son of God as well as the Son of Man (15:39).

C. So What?

What is the saving significance of Jesus Christ? According to Mark, the crucified and risen Jesus Christ assures his followers in every age that God will deliver us from life's obstacles, including death, and bring us into eternal life. Indeed, the risen Christ abides with us as we make our way across the sea of life (Mark 4:35-41). Although the Son of Man may seem to be "asleep" in the boat, he notices when we are hit by "a great windstorm" such as illness, unemployment, failure, depression, and injustice. We may cry as the disciples did, "Teacher, do you not care that we are perishing?" Yet he will rebuke "the wind" and say to "the sea, 'Peace! Be still!'" In the "dead calm" that ensues, the martyr-Messiah will say to us, "Why are you afraid? Have you still no faith?" Infused with hope, we may cope with our difficulties. We may ask again, "Who then is this, that even the wind and the sea obey him?" (4:41).

There are well-known Christians who have lived the Christian discipleship of Mark's gospel. St. Thérèse of Lisieux, known as the Little Flower, saw God's love at work in all situations, even during her doubt and her dying of tuberculosis. Martin Luther King Jr. and Rosa Parks opted for nonviolent action against racism, allowed this evil to crash on them, and ultimately advanced civil rights for minorities, especially for African Americans. Further, John Howard Griffin accepted the blindness that befell him, came "to see" the world anew, and went on to write *Black Like Me* (1961).[1] Also, the physicist Randy Pausch saw his life as a gift and an adventure, even while he was dying of cancer.[2]

II. St. Matthew on the Teacher-Messiah

St. Matthew likely wrote his gospel in AD 85 as his Jewish-Christian community was asking, are we betraying Moses and his teachings as we live in discipleship to Jesus Christ? In other words, what is involved in a life of right relationship with God, a life of righteousness? According to the evangelist Matthew, Jesus Christ is the new Moses, the teacher-Messiah (Matt 23:10), who taught by his words, deeds, and person that authentic religious practice opens our hearts, minds, and wills in love to God and to our neighbor in need. Indeed, faithfulness to God's covenant with Moses shows itself as we give food to the hungry, bring water to the thirsty, clothe the naked, care for the sick, and visit those in prison (Matt 25:31-46).

A. Jesus Christ, Living True Righteousness

"Who is your role model of an excellent teacher?" When asked this question, some of us think of television's Mr. Rogers. Fred Rogers, who hosted a children's show from 1968 to 2001, taught young people (and adults as well) with his puppets, stories, and learning activities. He even sang memorable songs such as "Won't You Be My Neighbor?" and "You Are Special." He began each show with his ritual of taking off his jacket, putting on his sweater, and replacing his shoes with his sneakers. Most importantly, he manifested the congruence of his person with his message. Having Mr. Rogers in mind is helpful when approaching Matthew's gospel with its portrait of Jesus Christ as the teacher-Messiah.

According to Matthew, Jesus praised those people "who hunger and thirst for righteousness" (Matt 5:6, 10). Indeed, he urged his listeners to "seek first the kingdom [of God] and his righteousness" (6:33). Jesus warned that "unless your righteousness exceeds that of the scribes and Pharisees, you will never enter the kingdom of heaven" (5:20). Condemning religious officials for whom righteousness meant external religious conformity, Jesus said, "I did not come to call the righteous but sinners" (9:13). True righteousness manifests itself in living the spirit or essence of the Mosaic laws, for example, in purity of heart or innocence (5:28), in love of one's enemies (5:44), and in going beyond the law of *talion* and even beyond the Golden Rule (5:38; 7:12). Consider too that Joseph, upon learning of Mary's pregnancy, remained committed to Mary and thus showed that he was "a righteous man" (1:19). At the Last Judgment, we will be judged on our righteousness as evinced in our care for the hungry, the thirsty, the naked, the ill, and the imprisoned (25:37, 46; cf. 10:41). Our religious practices should generate our right relationship with God as demonstrated in our love of neighbor (5:23-24).

B. Matthew's Literary Elements

Matthew did not write his narrative from scratch. Rather, he had at hand Mark's gospel as well as oral traditions with which Mark had not worked. Taking up these materials, he edited them into his portrait of Jesus Christ. In particular, the evangelist employed four literary elements.

First, Matthew clusters Jesus' teachings into five sermons or discourses, each of which ends with the expression "when Jesus had finished" (Matt 7:28; 11:1; 13:53; 19:1; 26:1). These five units represent the renewed "Pentateuch" of Jesus, the new Moses. According to this symbolism, God called Moses to teach the original Torah or Pentateuch, and God subsequently charged his Son, Jesus, to impart the renewed Torah, the teachings for the covenant of the heart of which the prophet Jeremiah spoke (Jer 31:31-34).

Second, the evangelist links Jesus with Moses by means of the image of a mountain. As Moses received and taught the Ten Commandments on Mount Sinai (Exod 19–20), Jesus "went up the mountain," where he declared his Beatitudes (Matt 5:1). Yet, according to Luke, Jesus gave his Beatitudes after he "came down" from a mountain and "stood on a level place" (Luke 6:17). Matthew also reports that after his resurrection Jesus directed his disciples "to the mountain," where he met them and commissioned them to "make disciples of all nations" (Matt 28:19).

Third, Matthew employs language of "fulfillment" as he writes about Jesus' words and deeds. Jesus was conceived in his mother by the Spirit in order "to fulfill" the words of Isaiah 7:14 concerning "Emmanuel" (Matt 1:22). The infant Jesus went with Joseph and Mary to Egypt and was then called by God, as Moses was, "out of Egypt" so that "what the Lord had said might be fulfilled" (2:15). Further, King Herod the Great's killing of infants "fulfilled" a saying by Jeremiah (2:17), and Jesus' childhood in Nazareth "fulfilled" what prophets had foretold (2:23). When Jesus began his ministry in Galilee, he "fulfilled" a prophecy of Isaiah (4:14). In his preaching, Jesus insisted that he came "not to abolish the law or the prophets. I have come not to abolish but to fulfill" (5:17). When the priests used Judas's money to purchase the potter's field, they "fulfilled what had been spoken through the prophet Jeremiah" (27:9). This repetition of "fulfill" conveys Matthew's conviction that Jesus brought to maturity what God had communicated to the people of Israel through "the law" and "the prophets." Jesus is the new Moses who "fulfilled" or realized the full meaning of what Moses and the prophets had previously communicated.

Fourth, Matthew describes the suffering, death, and resurrection of Jesus Christ in light of the story of the righteous person in the Wisdom of Solomon 2:1–3:8. This biblical text highlights the truth that most of us get annoyed at someone who insists on always telling the truth and persistently tries to do the right thing; for example, we're uneasy around whistle-blowers. Interestingly, in the fourth century BC, Socrates observed that in every society "the just man" will threaten the status quo. If this person persists in seeking justice, he "will be crucified"; see Plato's *Republic*, book II, no. 361e. Similarly, the Wisdom of

Solomon tells of "the ungodly" who scheme against anyone who is a "*righteous man*." (The words in italics in the previous sentence and below show the similarities between Wisdom 2:1–3:8 and Matthew 27:1–28:16.)

According to the Wisdom of Solomon, "the ungodly" will say among themselves, "Let us lie in wait for the *righteous man*, because he is inconvenient to us and opposes our actions" (Wis 2:12). These self-seeking people get upset when a good person "professes to have knowledge of God, and calls himself *a child of the Lord*" (2:13). They become enraged when he "calls the last end of the *righteous* happy, and boasts that *God is his father*" (2:16). Moved by anger, they plot against the person who is good. "Let us see if his words are true . . . ; for *if the righteous man is God's child, he will help him, and will deliver him from the hand of his adversaries*" (2:17-18). They say, "*Let us test him with insult and torture. . . . Let us condemn him to a shameful death, for, according to what he says, he will be protected [by God]*" (2:19-20). The ungodly will even put a righteous or just person to death. They themselves will eventually die and remain in "the devil's" company (2:24). "But the souls of *the righteous are in the hand of God*, and no torment will ever touch them" (3:1). As innocent people suffer, "their hope is full of *immortality*" (3:4). Indeed, they "will receive great reward" (3:5): they "*will govern the nations and rule over peoples*" (3:8).

This story of the persecuted righteous or innocent person has shaped Matthew's passion narrative. According to the evangelist, when Judas "saw that Jesus was condemned, he repented and brought back" the money that the priests had paid him. He said to the priests, "I have sinned in betraying *innocent blood*" (Matt 27:3-4). Then he "went off and hanged himself" (27:5). Meanwhile, Jesus had been brought to Pilate, who questioned him. But Pilate received a message from his wife: "Have nothing to do with that *innocent man*, for today I have suffered a great deal because of a dream about him" (27:19). Pilate himself saw that Jesus was indeed innocent. But knowing that the chief priests and the elders wanted Jesus executed, Pilate "washed his hands before the crowd, saying: 'I am *innocent* of this man's blood; see to it yourselves'" (27:24). Acting on Pilate's orders, soldiers crucified Jesus. Then, as Jesus was dying on the cross, the priests, scribes, and elders "*were mocking him*, saying: "He saved others; he cannot save himself. . . . *He trusts in God; let God deliver him now, if he wants to; for he said, 'I am God's Son'*" (27: 42-43). After Jesus died, he was buried in

Joseph of Arimathea's "new tomb." After three days, the women went to Jesus' tomb. Finding it empty, they learned from an "angel" that Jesus "*has been raised*" (28:6). Then Jesus himself "met them" (28:9). Later, when the disciples gathered on the mountain in Galilee, Jesus "came and said to them, '*All authority in heaven and on earth has been given to me*'" (28:18).

Matthew intentionally worked with the book of Wisdom's story of the righteous person and also adopted some of Wisdom's vocabulary as he recounted Jesus' suffering, death, and resurrection. By doing so, he reinforced his portrait of Jesus as the teacher-Messiah of true righteousness—the teacher who handed on the renewed "Pentateuch," taught on a mountain, and "fulfilled" Moses' words.

C. So What?

According to Matthew, Jesus has taught true righteousness. By his words, actions, and person, he taught that our love of God shows itself as we love our neighbor in need. Today, enabled and guided by the new Moses, we live in right relationship with God as we care for the hungry, the thirsty, the naked, the sick, and the imprisoned. In this, we heed Jesus' "Great Commission": "Go therefore and make disciples of all nations, baptizing them in the name of the Father and of the Son and the Holy Spirit, and teaching them to obey everything that I have commanded you. And remember, I am with you always, to the end of the age" (Matt 28:19-20).

Who are well-known Christians who have lived the true righteousness spoken of in Matthew's gospel? St. Francis of Assisi received clothing, food, and money from the wealthy and distributed these gifts to widows, beggars, and orphans. Mother Teresa of Calcutta went every day into the streets and cared for the men, women, and children who were ill and dying of hunger, disease, and violence. At Catholic Worker Houses in major United States cities, Dorothy Day offered food, clothing, and shelter to the homeless, the unemployed, and the abused. These three disciples are aptly described with Jesus' words: "Truly I tell you, just as you did it to one of the least of these who are members of my family, you did it to me" (Matt 25:40).

III. St. Luke on the Envoy-Messiah

Writing his gospel and the Acts of the Apostles in about AD 85, St. Luke identified Jesus Christ in relation to Luke's community with its increasing diversity of race, ethnicity, gender, and social status. According to Luke, the Lord Jesus is God's envoy-Messiah who has released the Spirit of reconciliation and peace in our pluralistic world. As in Jesus' parable of the Good Samaritan (Luke 10:29-37), we are called in the Spirit of Jesus to assist people whom we are prone to avoid or to exclude from our lives.

A. Jesus Christ, Releasing the Spirit of Reconciliation

In Luke's portrait, Jesus Christ is intent on making a journey from Nazareth to Jerusalem—a journey during which he frees or bestows the Spirit of healing and forgiveness among such marginal people as widows, children, the poor, and Samaritans. Jesus is similar to the American folk hero Johnny "Appleseed" Chapman, who in the early nineteenth century rode on horseback through western Pennsylvania, Ohio, and Indiana, giving out apple seeds and also preaching the Bible. But whereas Johnny Appleseed distributed apple seeds, Jesus Christ is God's ambassador offering us the Spirit who unites the world's diverse people with God and with one another.

B. Luke's Literary Elements

Luke assembled and edited materials from the oral traditions and was likely guided by Mark's gospel. In his endeavor, he employed at least four literary elements.

First, Luke mentions the Holy Spirit more often than the other evangelists do. According to Luke (and to Matthew), the Lord Jesus was conceived when the Spirit came upon Mary (Luke 1:35). Further, in his youth he was "filled with wisdom" (2:40, 52). At Jesus' baptism, the Spirit "descended upon him in bodily form like a dove" (3:22). Soon afterward, "Jesus, filled with the Holy Spirit, returned from the Jordan and was led by the Spirit into the desert" (4:1), where he resisted the devil's temptations. Subsequently, "Jesus, filled with the power of the Spirit, returned to Galilee" (4:14) and began to teach the people. In Nazareth's synagogue, he read aloud from the book of Isaiah: "The Spirit of the Lord is upon me because he has anointed me to bring good news to the poor . . . [and] to proclaim the year of the Lord's favor" (4:18-19; Isa 61:1-2). Next he walked around Galilee, teaching "the word of God" (5:1), calling his disciples (5:2-11), and curing people of their ills, for "the power [Spirit] of the Lord was with him for healing" (5:17). He restored to health people "who were tormented by unclean spirits" (6:18). Once, after he healed a woman with a hemorrhage, he said that "power [Spirit] had gone out from me" (8:46). Later, Jesus gave his disciples "authority . . . over all the power of the enemy" (10:19), and he "rejoiced in the Holy Spirit" (10:21). After Jesus went to Jerusalem, he permitted the authorities to execute him. As he took his last breath, he prayed, "Father, into your hands I commend my spirit" (23:46). After his resurrection, the risen Jesus came to his disciples and told them to remain in Jerusalem "until you are clothed with power [the Spirit] from on high" (24:49). As he promised, the Spirit came upon them on Pentecost (Acts 2:4). Luke's Acts of the Apostles narrates how the apostles and disciples traveled throughout the Roman Empire, releasing the Holy Spirit wherever they went, even in Rome itself.

Second, Luke frequently applies to Jesus the title "Lord." He does so most likely because "Lord" connotes varying forms and degrees of respect and hence has universal usage in relation to Jesus Christ. Since the title can refer to God, Jesus tells Satan, "Do not put the Lord, your God, to the test" (Luke 4:12). Yet it can also mean "Messiah." For example, after Jesus made it possible for Simon Peter to catch "many fish," Peter "fell down at Jesus' knees, saying, 'Go away from me, Lord, for I am a sinful man'" (5:6-8). Further, "Lord" can function in the sense of "Sir" and "Holy One." A man with leprosy uses the title in this sense: "Lord, if you wish, you can make me clean" (5:13). Gentiles too address Jesus as "Lord" in the sense of "Sir" or "Holy One." After Jesus set off to heal a centurion's slave, the official sent word to Jesus: "Lord, do not trouble yourself, for I am not worthy to have you come under my roof'" (7:6). Finally, in light of Jesus' resurrection appearances, the disciples refer to Jesus as the "Lord," the "Messiah": "The Lord has risen indeed, and he has appeared to Simon!" (24:34).

Third, Luke designs his narrative with the literary motif of a journey. According to Luke, after Jesus was conceived, Mary and Joseph made the journey from Nazareth to Bethlehem (Luke 2:4); then, after his birth, they and Jesus returned to Nazareth (3:9). During his public ministry, when the villagers of Capernaum tried "to prevent him from leaving them," Jesus explained that he is a wayfarer: "I must proclaim the good news of the kingdom of God to the other cities also; I was sent for this purpose" (4:42-43). After proclaiming his message throughout Galilee, Jesus "set his face to go to Jerusalem" (9:51). Going south through Samaria, Jesus communicated his "good news" among the Samaritans, whom most Jews shunned. Entering Judah with his disciples, Jesus began the last phase of his mission: "He went on ahead, going up to Jerusalem" (19:28). In the city of David, Jesus interacted with various types of people, including the scribes and the priests who had him put to death. After his resurrection, he appeared to his disciples and assured them that the Spirit would come upon them (24:49). As Luke reports in the Acts of the Apostles, after the disciples received the Spirit on Pentecost (Acts 1:5), they embarked on their journeys, of which the foremost was Paul's journey to Rome, the center of the empire.

Fourth, Luke alludes to the image of the messianic prophet in Isaiah 61:1-2 as he recounts Jesus' passion, death, and resurrection (Luke 23:28–24:49). (The words in italics below show the similarities between these two biblical texts.) In doing this, Luke implicitly draws on his earlier account of how Jesus inaugurated his public ministry in Nazareth's synagogue. On that occasion, according to Luke, Jesus "stood up to read, and the scroll of the prophet Isaiah was given to him." Then he read aloud: "The *Spirit* of the Lord is upon me, because he has *anointed me* to bring *good news* to the poor. He has sent me to proclaim *release to the captives* and recovery of sight to the blind, to let *the oppressed go free*, to proclaim the year of the Lord's favor" (Luke 4:17-19; cf. Isa 61:1-2). These two verses conclude in Isaiah with a third verse: "To provide for those who *mourn in Zion [Jerusalem]*—to give them a garland instead of ashes, the oil of *gladness [good news] instead of mourning*, the mantle of praise instead of *a faint spirit*" (Isa 61:3).

Notice how Isaiah's words resonate in Luke's account of Jesus' passion, death, and resurrection (Luke 23:28–24:49). According to Luke, Jesus, while bearing his cross through the streets, comforts the women who are *mourning*: "*Daughters of Jerusalem, do not weep for me, but weep for yourselves and for your children*" (23:28). Shortly thereafter, Jesus spiritually frees the soldiers who were *oppressed* into Rome's military service: "*Father, forgive them; for they do not know what they are doing*" (23:34). Then Jesus proclaims "*release to the captives*" as he says to the "Good Thief," "Truly I tell you, today you will be with me in Paradise" (23:43). Further, as he is about to die, Jesus prays, "*Father, into your hands I commend my spirit,"* and, in doing so, he gives back to the Father *"the spirit of the Lord,"* which he had received at his conception (23:46; cf. 1:35). Finally, according to Luke, the risen Jesus promises his disciples that they will be *"clothed with power [the Spirit] from on high"* (24:49). In other words, they will have their *"faint spirit"* replaced with *"the mantle of praise."* On Pentecost, as Luke reports, the divine "power" came upon Jesus' followers: *"All of them were filled with the Holy Spirit and began to speak in other languages, as the Spirit gave them ability"* (Acts 2:4).

In sum, Luke portrays Jesus Christ as God's envoy of the Spirit of reconciliation, of "salvation" to "all peoples" (Luke 2:31). The evangelist achieves this portrait by emphasizing the Holy Spirit, using the title "Lord," relying on the journey motif, and weaving in Isaiah's image of God's messianic prophet (Isa 61:1-2; Luke 4:18-19).

C. So What?

Sad to say, bridge builders or reconcilers often enrage the people whom they want to help. St. Kateri Tekakwitha was rejected by some of her Algonquin and Iroquois kin because of her Christian faith and her decision not to marry. President Abraham Lincoln was assassinated by the Confederate sympathizer John Wilkes Booth, even though Lincoln labored to heal the wounds of division between the South and the North. Mohandas Gandhi was killed by a fellow Hindu because he was promoting respect and civil rights for Muslims in India. Malcolm X was gunned down by his former associates in the Black Muslims because he returned from Mecca with the message of the "universal brotherhood" in Allah of all people, regardless of race. Yitzhak Rabin, Israel's prime minister, was assassinated by an Israeli fanatic because he was seeking ways to include Palestinians in the State of Israel. Today, Sister Helen Prejean, CSJ, is ridiculed by some people because of her efforts to reconcile convicted murderers on death row with their victims' families; see the book and movie *Dead Man Walking.* The bearers of the Spirit of unity often meet stiff resistance and even hatred, especially within their own communities.

As presented by Luke, the Lord Jesus in the Spirit is intent on transforming us as he heals us of our infirmities (e.g., as with the woman with the hemorrhage; Luke 8:40-56), casts out our demons (e.g., as with the Gerasene demoniac; Luke 8:26-39), reknits our ties with other people (e.g., as with the tax collector Zaccheus; Luke 19:1-10), and reconciles us with the Father (e.g., as with the Good Thief on the cross; Luke 23:39-43). Moreover, the envoy-Messiah urges us, as he charged the seventy disciples, to promote communities of forgiveness, healing, and reconciliation among all people (Luke 10:1-12). As in the parable of the Good Samaritan (10:29-37), we are to bind up the wounds of others, especially of the victims on society's margins. We are called to form a new kind of community, established not according to the *pax Romana* or the *pax Americana* but according to the *pax Christi*, as proclaimed by the angels at Jesus' birth: "On earth peace among those whom [God] favors" (2:14).

IV. St. John on the Good-Shepherd–Messiah

Writing in AD 90, St. John was intent on identifying Jesus Christ for John's community as it experienced opposition from some Jewish officials, "the Jews" (John 7:13), and also from society, "the world" (14:17). According to John, Jesus is "the Messiah, the Son of God, the one coming into the world" (11:27; 20:31). He is the Good Shepherd who has entered "the sheepfold" and now "calls his own sheep by name and leads them out" (10:1-3). The risen Christ, the Good Shepherd, is still among us, calling us by name and imparting the Spirit so that we, like Nicodemus and the Samaritan woman, may be "born from above" (3:3; 4:29).

A. Jesus Christ, God's Word Incarnate

One of the most Christ-like figures in modern literature is Billy Budd in Herman Melville's novella of the same name. This British sailor possesses the honesty, fairness, and helpfulness that endear him to the ship's crew and to its Captain Vere. However, these same qualities enrage the ship's master-at-arms, John Claggert, who resents that the sailors respect Budd but not Claggert, their official leader. Asserting his power, Claggert falsely charges Budd of plotting a mutiny. At a hearing, Budd tries to respond to this allegation, but he gets flustered because of his speech impediment and strikes Claggert, accidentally killing him. An official court-martial ensues. Even though Captain Vere and the ship's officers privately acknowledge Budd's innocence, they fear that they will lose their power over the ship's crew if they are lenient with Billy Budd. Thus, they declare that Budd is guilty of murder. Hanged from the ship's yardarm, Budd dies uttering words of forgiveness: "God bless Captain Vere!"

The story of Billy Budd affords a way into John's gospel. The ship's crew is attracted to Billy Budd because of his truthfulness, fairness, and generosity. Similarly, in John's gospel the people who yearn for truth, justice, and love are drawn to Jesus Christ, who is God's Word made flesh (John 1:14). As Wisdom Incarnate, Jesus Christ embodies truth, justice, and love—the transcendent yet immanent realities at the heart of creation. Jesus, like Billy Budd, is rejected by those self-seeking, influential individuals who, like John Claggert, want power over other people. Billy Budd dies a wrongful death on the yardarm, and Jesus dies an absurd death on the cross. Budd accepts his fate, and Jesus Christ says yes to his crucifixion, knowing that his selfless love, his agape, for God's people will clearly show itself on the cross. He declares, "No one has greater love than this, to lay down one's life for one's friends" (15:13).

B. St. John's Literary Elements

Although John creates his portrait of the good-shepherd–Messiah by means of numerous literary elements, we'll consider only two: John's literary design and his account of Jesus' passion, death, and resurrection.

The gospel consists of two units. In the first unit, Jesus "calls his own sheep by name," and in the second, Jesus "leads them out" (John 10:3). In the first unit, called the "Book of Signs" (1:19–12:50), Jesus performs seven miracles or "signs" (2:11; 11:47), such as turning water into wine at Cana (2:1-12) and healing the Gentile official's son at Capernaum (4:43-54). In response to Jesus' signs and teachings, people in search of truth, justice, and love come to believe in him as God's Son, as the Good Shepherd whom they choose to follow "because they know his voice" (10:4). They include Nicodemus (3:1-21), the Samaritan woman (4:1-42), and the man born blind (9:1-41). Reacting against Jesus' signs and teachings, the people in power hate Jesus. They include some Jewish officials who want either to stone Jesus (8:59; 10:31) or to arrest him so that Pontius Pilate can put him to death (11:57).

In the gospel's second unit, called the "Book of Glory" (John 13:1–20:31), Jesus "leads out" (10:3) his sheep so that "they may have life, and have it abundantly" (10:10). That is, he tells his followers about the Father and Jesus Christ's selfless love for them: "Just as I have loved you, you also should love one another (13:34). He also assures them that the Father and he will send them "another Advocate," the "Spirit of truth" (14:16-17). Further, Jesus symbolically shows his selfless love as he washes the disciples' feet (13:1-38). Then he reveals the infinite depths of divine agape as he undergoes his passion, death, and resurrection (18:1–19:42). Thus he is the true Messiah: "I am the good shepherd. The good shepherd lays down his life for the sheep" (10:11). Then Jesus' crucifixion and burial are followed by his resurrection and his appearances to the disciples (20:1–21:25). In Jesus' words: "I lay down my life in order to take it up again" (10:17). As the evangelist said at the outset, "And the Word became flesh and lived among us, and we have seen his glory, the glory of the father's only son, full of grace and truth" (1:14).

A second literary element that shapes John's portrait of the Good Shepherd is the evangelist's reliance on the book of Proverbs in which divine Wisdom is personified (Prov 1:20-23). As such, Wisdom gives a discourse that begins, "To you, O people, I *call*" (Prov 8:1; the added italics here and below show the textual similarities). Similarly, in John's gospel Jesus Christ "*calls* his own sheep by name" (John 10:3). In Proverbs, Wisdom adds, "Hear, for I will speak *noble things*, and from my lips will come *what is right*; my mouth will utter *truth*" (Prov 8:4-7). Further, Wisdom states, "By me *kings* reign, and *rulers* decree what is just" (Prov 8:15). However, Pontius Pilate did not govern with Wisdom, as evidenced in his failure to recognize Jesus as truth embodied (John 19:38). Hence, Pilate does not recognize the voice of the Good Shepherd (John 10:4). Yet Nicodemus and the Samaritan woman perceive Jesus' true identity. To them Wisdom's words apply: "I love those who love me, and those who seek me diligently find me" (Prov 8:17). In Proverbs, Wisdom preceded creation: "The LORD created me *at the beginning* of his work, the first of his acts of long ago" (Prov 8:22). Alluding to these words, St. John's gospel begins, "*In the beginning* was the Word, and the Word was with God, and the Word was God" (John 1:1). Finally, in Proverbs, Wisdom observes that "whoever finds me *finds life* and obtains favor from the LORD" (Prov 8:35). Wisdom's assurance comes to the Good Shepherd's lips: "I came that they may have *life*, and have it abundantly" (John 10:10).

Now consider John's passion narrative. When Jesus comes before Pilate, Pilate asks him, "So you are a *king?*" And Jesus answers: "You say that I am a *king*. For this I was born, . . . to testify to the *truth*. Everyone who belongs to the *truth* listens to my voice." Pilate asks him, "What is *truth*?" (John 18:37-38). Pilate's question evinces his character: because he does not seek the truth, he does not recognize Jesus as Wisdom Incarnate. Next Jesus is brought before the crowd; he is wearing *the crown* of thorns and royalty's *purple robe*. Pilate declares, "Here is *the man*!" Since Jesus' opponents do not seek Wisdom, the true shepherd, they shout, "Crucify him!" (19:5-6). Pilate has Jesus scourged and again brought before the crowd. He declares, "Here is your *King*!" The people shout: "Away with him! Away with him! Crucify him! . . . We have no *king* but the emperor" (19:14-15). Once again, Jesus' enemies show that they do not seek Wisdom. After Jesus is crucified, Pilate has affixed to the cross the inscription "Jesus of Nazareth, the *King* of the Jews" (19:20). Paradoxically, the crucified Jesus is truly the king; he is the Wisdom that should guide all people, especially religious and political leaders. But the Word Incarnate was not recognized by the religious and civil officials, Caiaphas and Pilate, even when he was standing in front of them.

In John's gospel, Jesus appears after his resurrection first to Mary Magdalene. Although she does not initially recognize him, she immediately knows him when he calls her name as the Good Shepherd calls each sheep "by name" (John 20:16; 10:3). She is a true disciple because she knows the Good Shepherd's "voice." (10:4). After recounting some of Jesus' resurrection appearances, the evangelist clarifies that he told Jesus' story "so that you may come to believe that Jesus is the *Messiah*, the *Son of God*, and that through believing you may *have life* in his name" (20:31). Thus, John's aim is to lead us to Wisdom: "For whoever finds me *finds life* and obtains favor from the LORD" (Prov 8:25).

C. So What?

According to the evangelist, Jesus Christ now lives with the Father beyond death and evil, and he and the Father are sending us the "Advocate," the "Spirit of truth" (John 14:16-17). Near the end of his earthly life, Jesus prayed that the Father would send us the Spirit: "Sanctify them in the truth; your word is truth" (17:17). Today the Holy Spirit is intent on inspiring and guiding us, as the Spirit inspired and guided John's community, to hear the voice of the Good Shepherd, Wisdom Incarnate, who is "the way, the truth, and the life" (14:6). For our part, we must heed Jesus' words to Nicodemus: "You must be born from above. . . . So it is with everyone who is born of the Spirit" (3:7-8). Drawn by the Spirit toward the truth, justice, and love (16:13), we undergo *metanoia* and strive to live selfless love similar to the agape that Jesus lived as he cared for people such as Lazarus (11:1-57) and as he allowed himself to be crucified by Pontius Pilate (13:1-15; 18:36-38). As we witness to the Word made flesh, we may lead people to "the Savior of the world," as the Samaritan woman did (4:42). But we may also find ourselves reviled as the blind man was by some officials after he claimed to have received his sight from Jesus (9:35).

Who are well-known people who have selflessly lived for Wisdom, as envisioned by the evangelist John? In Spain, St. Teresa of Ávila responded to the Spirit as she became a mystic, reformed the Carmelite Order, and, despite the objections of the Inquisition, attested to the human journey to God in her classic *The Interior Castle*. In the US, Eleanor Roosevelt dedicated herself to the well-being of women, children, and minorities; she was ahead of her time in calling for equal pay regardless of gender, for child-care facilities, and for better housing for the poor. In South Africa, Nelson Mandela advocated for the end of apartheid, was imprisoned for twenty-six years, but was eventually elected South Africa's president. In India, the Dalai Lama has resided in exile since 1959 and has become an international luminary for compassion, honesty, and human rights. In their respective ways, these four people have devoted themselves to Wisdom; to them Jesus' words apply: "But those who do what is true come to the light, so that it may be clearly seen that their deeds have been done in God" (John 3:21).

V. Jesus Christ, the Key to Personal Wholeness

On the way to Caesarea Philippi, Jesus asked his disciples, "But who do you say that I am?" (Mark 8:29). Today, the crucified and risen Jesus continues to pose this question to us. Christ in the Spirit invites God's people to know and love more fully God's Word, Wisdom, who "became flesh and lived among us" (John 1:14). The crucified and risen Christ in the Spirit persistently asks us who we say that he is. He poses this question in order to orient us not only to the mystery of the Father, the Son, and the Holy Spirit but also to the mystery of ourselves. As we come to know the Word Incarnate more fully, we simultaneously discover ourselves more fully. The living Christ is the key to our personal wholeness; he is our Savior and our salvation (see Vatican II's *Gaudium et Spes* 10).

As we have seen, each of the four canonical gospels conveys its own portrait of Jesus Christ. In Mark's gospel, Jesus is the Son of God, the martyr-Messiah, who underwent his passion, death, and resurrection in order to establish God's reign in human affairs. In Matthew's gospel, Jesus is the new Moses, the teacher-Messiah, who has realized and communicated to us our right relationship with God by means of his words and deeds as well as by his suffering, death, and resurrection. In Luke's gospel and the Acts of the Apostles, Jesus is the Lord, the envoy-Messiah, who has released the Holy Spirit among us by means of his paschal mystery. Finally, in John's gospel, Jesus Christ is God's Word, Wisdom Incarnate, the good-shepherd–Messiah, who selflessly came among us, laid down his life in self-sacrificing love, rose to new life, and sent "the Spirit of truth" among us so that we may enter into God's sheepfold.

These four distinct, though interrelated, portraits of Jesus Christ prompt three observations concerning Jesus Christ and ourselves.

First, the four gospels attest that Jesus Christ is a singular mystery. Indeed, whereas each of us is a human mystery, Christ is the divine-human mystery. While every human person as a human mystery can be the subject of more than one identifying depiction, Jesus Christ as the divine-human mystery is rightly the subject of countless portraits in the New Testament, the Christian tradition, and the church. Thus, we pray that we may again and again "declare the mystery of Christ" (Col 4:3).

Second, although the four gospels provide differing portraits of Jesus Christ, they agree that the culminating "event" of the Lord's passion, death, and resurrection decisively reveals who Jesus Christ is and also what Christ has done and still does for us. This climax in the four canonical gospels manifests that the Lord Jesus is God's Son and the Savior of all people. For this reason, the paschal mystery is the essence of the church's Good News. It is succinctly expressed in the teaching that St. Paul received at his conversion in AD 34: "That Christ died for our sins in accordance with the scriptures, and that he was buried, and that he was raised on the third day in accordance with the scriptures, and that he appeared to Cephas, then to the twelve" (1 Cor 15:3-5). If this extraordinary Good News is not true, then—as St. Paul declared—"your faith is futile and you are still in your sins" (15:17).

Third, the four gospels generate portraits of Jesus Christ through which we can increasingly know and love the Lord Jesus alive in the Spirit and simultaneously discover ourselves as God envisions us. The gospels of Mark, Matthew, Luke, and John present Jesus Christ in the Spirit as the divine-human mystery who possesses full personal wholeness and is hence the source of our salvation, our self-realization as God intends us. In other words, the living Christ is God's gift of *salus*. As we live in relation to Wisdom, the Word Incarnate, we can discover our true selves in union with God and in communion with one another and all of creation. As we encounter Christ in our lives and in the church, we find that "he is the image of the invisible God, *the firstborn* of all creation; for in him all things in heaven and on earth were created, things visible and invisible, whether thrones or dominions or rulers or powers—all things have been created through him and for him" (Col 1:16; italics added).

That Jesus Christ is the Savior, the key to our personal wholeness, is clearly conveyed in the book of Revelation. According to the Bible's last book, Jesus Christ is the bearer of our salvation because, having overcome evil and death and meaninglessness, he now unites us in the Spirit with the Father. The Lord is "the faithful witness, *the firstborn* of the dead, and the ruler of the kings of the earth" (Rev 1:5; italics added). Let us now turn to the book of Revelation so that we may glimpse the New Jerusalem to which our life journeys may take us.

Chapter 8

Salvation

The Gift Fulfilled in God

When Christians pray, we often make the "sign of the cross" with the words "In the name of the Father and of the Son and of the Holy Spirit." In doing this, we engage in a ritual that began with the baptism of the first Christians (Matt 28:19).

But what does this symbol mean? Even though we may hurry as we make the sign of the cross, we sense that this simple prayer possesses great significance, that it declares something about God and about ourselves in relation to God. What in particular are we acknowledging when we trace a cross with our hands from our foreheads to our chests and to each of our shoulders and simultaneously speak the divine names that were said over us at baptism?

An ancient answer to this question is available in the book of Revelation, also known as the Apocalypse (Greek, *apo*, "away from," + *kaluptein*, "to cover"; hence, "to uncover," "to reveal"), written by John of Patmos in AD 95. Located at the end of the Bible, this text is often cited today by people who predict the imminent arrival of God's Last Judgment. However, the book of Revelation is not a crystal ball that foretells disaster. Rather, it is an intricate tapestry of images meant to depict God's salvation in and beyond history. This imaginative biblical book was meant not to fuel anxiety but to nurture the hope that God will bring faithful people beyond evil, meaninglessness, and death to *salus*, to personal wholeness, in Christ through the Holy Spirit.

Among Revelation's numerous images, there is one in particular that sums up the book's assurance of God's salvific presence and action in our lives. Moreover, this image was one wellspring for the early church's ritual of the sign of the cross. This is the image of "the river of the *water of life*, bright as crystal, flowing from the *throne of God* and of the *Lamb* through the middle of the street of the city" (Rev 22:1-2; italics added). This graphic depiction of the one divine throne with the Almighty, the water of life, and the Lamb richly contributed to the church's belief in the triune God.[1]

This chapter studies the book of Revelation in order to shed more light on the mystery of God and on the mystery of our lives in God's presence. In this inquiry, we reflect on Revelation's images of God and of our salvation. As we do so, we should remember St. Thomas Aquinas's insight that "we cannot know what God is" (*Summa Theologiae*, I, 9, 3). In other words, because God is the ultimate mystery, we can increasingly understand God, but we can never fully fathom God. Similarly, we are inexhaustible realities whom we can increasingly know but never fully comprehend. With the psalmist, we must confess, "Such knowledge is too wonderful for me; it is so high that I cannot attain it" (Ps 139:6).

I. God and Our Salvation

The religious experience of the Czech playwright Václav Havel (October 5, 1936–December 18, 2011) can facilitate our entry into the book of Revelation. Although Havel did not formally practice the Catholic faith into which he was baptized as an infant, he thought long and hard about the mystery of God and human life. In fact, he often discussed Christian belief with active Catholics, even though the church was suppressed in Czechoslovakia, a state within the USSR from 1948 until 1989. At the age of forty-four, Havel had a transcendent encounter similar to what John of Patmos described in Revelation.

This religious experience occurred during Havel's imprisonment. On October 23, 1979, Václav Havel was sentenced to four and one-half years in prison because he signed a declaration of human rights called Charter 77. He was, of course, distressed by his incarceration. Yet, after a few months, he received a vision or a moment outside of time and space, which he subsequently described in a letter to his wife Olga:

> Again, I call to mind that distant moment in Hermanice when on a hot, cloudless day, I sat on a pile of rusty iron and gazed into the crown of an enormous tree that stretched, with dignified repose, up and over all the fences, wires, bars and watchtowers that separated

me from it. As I watched the imperceptible trembling of its leaves against an endless sky, I was overcome by a sensation that is difficult to describe: all at once, I seemed to rise above all the coordinates of my momentary existence in the world into a kind of state outside time in which all the beautiful things I had ever seen and experienced existed in a total "co-present"; I felt a sense of reconciliation, indeed of an almost gentle consent to the inevitable course of things as revealed to me now, and this combined with a carefree determination to face what had to be faced.[2]

Václav Havel's description of his religious experience is crucial for understanding his subsequent personal strength and vision of life. His encounter with God, or "Being," to use Havel's term, nurtured the poet's hope so that he not only endured his imprisonment but also went on to serve, after the collapse of the Soviet Union in 1989, as the last president of Czechoslovakia (1989–92) and the first president of the Czech Republic (1992–2003). Further, Havel's account of his transcendent encounter is an appropriate entry into Revelation with its bewildering testimony to God's saving presence and action in our lives.

A. The Author, Context, and Literary Elements of the Book of Revelation

Although the book of Revelation was immediately intelligible to early Christians, it opens its wisdom to us today when we approach it on the basis of critical study as well as prayerful reflection and discussion in the church. At the outset, we must appreciate the author's historical context and intention as well as the book's literary elements.

John of Patmos wrote Revelation near the end of Emperor Domitian's persecution (AD 81–96) of Christians in Asia Minor, today's Turkey. Similar to Václav Havel, who was imprisoned for upholding human rights, John was exiled to the island of Patmos because he opposed Rome's oppression of Christians (Rev 1:9). Also, like Havel, it was during his isolation that John received his visions; that is, he "was in the spirit on the Lord's day" (1:10).

After Revelation's prologue (Rev 1:1-20), John of Patmos develops his testimony in six units. First, he writes seven letters to seven churches in Asia Minor (2:1–3:22). Second, he recounts his vision of the Almighty and the Lamb enthroned in heaven (4:1–5:14) as well as his visions of the seven seals and of the seven trumpets (6:1–11:19). Third, John witnesses to the heavenly signs of the woman, the dragon, the beasts, and the Lamb (12:1–14:20) and also to the plagues and bowls (15:1–16:21). Fourth, he recalls his visions of the "great whore" (Rome) and God's judgment of "Babylon" (Rome; 17:1–18:24). Fifth, the author describes his visions of the victory of Christ, the judgment of the dead, and the defeat of evil (19:1–20:15). Sixth, he recounts his vision of "a new heaven and a new earth" with the arrival of the New Jerusalem on earth (21:1–22:5). In Revelation's epilogue (22:6-21), John exhorts his readers to live with hope in the coming of God's kingdom and of Jesus Christ.

Running through John's testimony is the message of assurance: through his life, death, and resurrection, Jesus Christ, "the Lamb," has already conquered evil, meaninglessness, and death (Rev 5:6-14). He has realized in himself God's kingdom, God's new age of truth, justice, and love. Thus, Christ himself is the divine promise or covenant that God will eventually destroy the world's corrupt powers as God had previously humbled the Babylonian Empire (14:8; 18:2) and that God will establish the new creation in which the Lamb will wed the bride, "the new Jerusalem" (21:1-2). Until that day, God's faithful people must live with "love, faith, service, and patient endurance" (2:19). We must continually pray, "Come, Lord Jesus!" (22:20). St. Paul too had prayed, "Our Lord, come!" (1 Cor 16:22).

John of Patmos opted to convey his message of hope in the literary genre of an apocalyptic text (see chap. 5). Consonant with this form, the book's images and symbols cryptically function in reference to the specific rulers, empires, and situations with which its contemporary Christians were familiar. For example, the "woman clothed with the sun" (Rev 12:1) is a polyvalent symbol, simultaneously representing the Jewish people from whom came the Blessed Mother Mary, Jesus Christ, and the church. Further, the "beast rising out of the sea" (13:1) likely symbolizes the Roman Empire, and the "beast that rose out of the earth" represents the Roman officials in Asia intent on compelling Christians to worship "Nero Caesar," whose number is 666 (13:18). Other numbers too have figurative meanings. For example, since the number seven means "perfection" or "countless," there are "seven churches," "seven seals," "seven visions," and "seven trumpets." Also, since the number twelve connotes "wholeness" or "completion," there are "twelve tribes" and "twelve kinds of fruit" on the tree, as well as "twenty-four elders" (2 x 12) before God's throne and "one hundred forty-four thousand" (12 x 12,000) faithful people (21:12; 22:2; 4:4; 7:4).

According to John of Patmos, the Christians of his day—and the Christians in every age, even today!—are living in the interim. On the one hand, God's reign has already begun. Jesus Christ has won the decisive battle by means of his life, death, and resurrection. The Lamb slain now abides on the divine throne (Rev 5:1-14). On the other hand, God's reign has not yet fully arrived. Jesus Christ has not yet engaged in the final battle with Satan (19:11-21). Jesus Christ's followers live their lives, therefore, between "the already" and "the not yet," and they should do so with the assurance of God's final victory for creation's complete well-being, its salvation. In this in-between time, Christians face an either-or choice: either they can live in theonomy, or they can revert to radical heteronomy and radical autonomy. If they remain true to the risen Christ, the Lamb slain, they may be misunderstood and perhaps persecuted by their contemporaries, yet they will eventually receive the fullness of God's *salus*. The Almighty, the Father, will gather the faithful people in the last age around the divine throne (20:12). The crucified and risen Lamb, the Son, will "guide them to springs of the water of life" (7:17) and will wed them (21:9). And the water of life, the Spirit, shall sustain them, join them to the tree of life, and nourish them to bear fruit (22:2). Thus, Christians will receive the Holy Spirit: "Let anyone who wishes take the water of life as a gift" (22:17).

B. The Marriage, the Divine Throne, and the Tree of Life

Let's return to Václav Havel's description of his religious experience. As Havel looked up into "the crown of an enormous tree," he was lifted "outside of time" and received "a sense of reconciliation" with "the inevitable course of things." He felt as though he were falling into the "mystery" of "Being": "A profound amazement at the sovereignty of Being became a dizzying sensation of tumbling endlessly into the abyss of its mystery; an unbounded joy at being alive. . . . I would even say I was somehow 'struck by love,' though I don't know precisely for whom or what."[3]

Havel's talk of being "outside of time" and "struck by love" is noteworthy, for John of Patmos also attests to being lifted out of time and awed by divine love. John expresses his sense of God's gracious love by means of the image of "the water of life, bright as crystal, flowing from the throne of God and of the Lamb" to "the tree of life with its twelve kinds of fruit" (Rev 22:1-2). Let's consider aspects of this rich imagery.

In a vision John saw "the throne of God and of the Lamb" (Rev 22:1) in the middle of Jerusalem where the second temple had stood. In God's last age, the holy city's "temple is the Lord God Almighty and the Lamb" (21:22). Moreover, the New Jerusalem has "no need of sun or moon to shine on it, for the glory of God is its light, and its lamp is the Lamb" (21:23). What is this "glory"? It is the divine communion of love, the selfless union of the Almighty and of the Lamb and of the water of life. God's agape radiates through the New Jerusalem. "The nations will walk by its light" (21:24).

John's view of God enthroned in Jerusalem (Rev 22:1; 21:22) builds on his earlier vision of "a throne, with one seated on the throne" (4:2). Moreover, "the one seated there looks like jasper and carnelian, and around the throne is a rainbow that looks like an emerald" (4:3). Surrounding the one enthroned, the Almighty, are "twenty-four elders, dressed in white robes," and coming from the throne are "seven flaming torches, which are the seven spirits of God," that is, the Holy Spirit. The Almighty is receiving praise and thanks from the heavenly host. In particular, "four living creatures"—a lion, an ox, a being with a human face, and an eagle—sing, "Holy, holy, holy, the Lord God the Almighty, who was and is and is to come." Simultaneously, the twenty-four elders are singing, "You are worthy, our Lord and God, to receive glory and honor and power, for you created all things, and by your will they existed and were created" (4:8-11).

This is not all. John also sees on the divine throne the crucified and risen Christ, the "Lamb standing as if it had been slaughtered" (Rev 5:6). This Lamb "went and took the scroll from the right hand of the one who was seated on the throne." Emanating from the Lamb are "the seven spirits of God," the Holy Spirit, "sent out into all the earth" (5:6). Immediately, the four living creatures and the twenty-four elders "fell before the Lamb," singing, "You are worthy to take the scroll and to open its seals, for you were slaughtered and by your blood you ransomed for God saints from every tribe and language and people and nation; you have made them to be a kingdom and priests serving our God" (5:9-10). Moreover, the angels chant, "Worthy is the Lamb that was slaughtered to receive power and wealth and wisdom and might and honor and glory and blessing!" (5:12). All creatures "in heaven and on earth" sing, "To the one seated on the throne and to the Lamb be blessing and honor and glory and might forever and ever!" (5:13).

Note that "the seven spirits of God" emanate from "the one enthroned" and also from "the Lamb" (Rev 4:5; 5:6). These "seven spirits" are the Holy Spirit, who is distinct from the Almighty and from the Lamb and yet is fully united with the Father and the Son. God is three "persons" in one "Being," according to the church's later teaching. Acknowledging this mystery, John begins Revelation with the threefold salutation "Grace to you and peace *from him who is and was and who is to come* [the Father], and from *the seven spirits* [the Holy Spirit] who are before his throne, and from *Jesus Christ* [the Lamb], the faithful witness, the firstborn of the dead, and the ruler of the kings of the earth" (1:4-5; italics added).

This depiction of the "throne" with the "one seated," the "Lamb," and the "seven spirits" witnesses to the paradoxical reality of God's personal differentiation in God's personal unity. As attested in Matthew's gospel, the one God is the Father and the Son and the Holy Spirit (Matt 28:19). The divine "persons" (as now spoken of in the church) are distinct, and yet they abide together on the one "throne," the single union of agape. (The theological name for this divine mystery is the "immanent Trinity.") However, while God fully exists in the divine life, God also freely chooses to offer salvation, *salus*, to creation and to the human family. The one enthroned—the Almighty, the Lamb, and the seven spirits—will eventually unite all faithful people in the union of divine love. (The theological name for this salvific mystery is the "economic Trinity.")

God's gracious outreach to us occurs through each of the divine "persons." Referring to the Almighty, an angel tells John of Patmos, "See, the home of God is among mortals. He will dwell with them; they will be his peoples, and God himself will be with them" (Rev 21:3). Shortly thereafter, the Almighty promises to send the Holy Spirit among all people: "To the thirsty I will give water as a gift from the water of life" (21:6). John then beholds the marriage of Christ and God's people. He attests that he "saw the holy city, the new Jerusalem, coming down out of heaven from God, prepared as a bride adorned for her husband" (21:2). Then an angel says to John, "Come, I will show you the bride, the wife of the Lamb" (21:9-10). At this, John sees the holy city in which there abides "the Lord God the Almighty and the Lamb" (21:22). Finally, John sees the union of the Holy Spirit and God's people. That is, he observes "the river of the water of life, bright as crystal, flowing from the throne of God and the Lamb through the middle of the street of the city" (22:1). God's saving love, the Spirit, is nourishing God's people.

John's image of the "tree of life" (Rev 22:2) has a twofold significance. First, according to the book of Genesis, the "tree of life" that God planted in the middle of the Garden of Eden (Gen 2:9) became off limits to human beings; after the sin of Adam and Eve, God "placed a sword flaming and turning to guard the way to the tree of life" (Gen 3:24). But—as foretold in Ezekiel 47—in God's end-time, the tree of life will stand in the middle of the holy city and be accessible to all people. Thus, according to John of Patmos, the Almighty has declared, "To everyone who conquers [through faithfulness to God], I will give permission to eat from the tree of life that is in the paradise of God" (Rev 2:7). In other words, God is offering *salus*, personal wholeness, to all people who are grafted to the tree of life.

Second, the tree of life, sustained by the water of life, is complete; it bears "twelve kinds of fruit, producing its fruit each month" (Rev 22:2). This image of the tree, nurtured by the Spirit, yielding a bountiful harvest alludes to the image of the fruitful vine in John's gospel. According to the evangelist St. John, Jesus taught, "I am the vine, you are the branches. Those who abide in me and I in them bear much fruit" (John 15:5). This image of the vine, Jesus Christ, bearing fruit is a crucial source for Revelation's image of the tree of life, the true vine, "producing its fruit each month" (Rev 22:2). In this perspective, the water of life, the Spirit, unites people with the crucified and risen Christ and nourishes them so that they in union with Christ "bear much fruit" (John 15:5; cf. Jer 17:7-8). According to the evangelist, Jesus taught, "My Father is glorified by this, that you bear much fruit and become my disciples" (15:8).

II. The Paradox of Love and Freedom

The meaning of Revelation's imagery opens further to us as we relate it again to Václav Havel's description of his religious experience. After recalling that he was "struck by love," Havel adds that his encounter with God had a paradoxical effect on him. On the one hand, it affirmed him and his convictions, and on the other hand, it united him with "Being." In other words, coming into God's presence had a twofold influence, nurturing his individuality and yet also joining him with "Being." It gave him "the experience of genuine 'contact,' but contact as something both autonomous and integral—[as] paradoxical as that may be."[4] Havel is speaking here of the paradox of love and freedom, the paradox of personal union and personal differentiation: the greater the love among persons, the greater the differentiation among these persons (see chap. 3). In the book of Revelation, John of Patmos witnesses to this paradox in God and also in the relationship between God and us.

A. Union and Differentiation in God

The book of Revelation attests to the paradox of love and freedom in God. On the one hand, it upholds God's unity, and on the other hand, it refers to God's three persons. Thus, this book has fueled the confession of belief that the church formulated in the Nicene Creed (AD 325 and AD 381): "I believe in one God, the Father almighty. . . . I believe in one Lord Jesus Christ. . . . I believe in the Holy Spirit, the Lord, the giver of life." In order to elucidate Revelation's understanding of the union and differentiation in the triune God, we'll employ the notions of the person as an "I," a "we," and a "doer"—that is, the person as a subject, a social being, and a self-agent (see chap. 1).

God is the divine "I." According to John of Patmos, there is one "throne" that unites the Almighty, the Lamb, and the water of life (Rev 4:2-3; 22:1). Moreover, both the Almighty and the Lamb self-identify as the one Source and Goal of creation and history. The Almighty declares, "I am the Alpha and the Omega" (1:8; 21:6). At the same time, the Lamb, the "Son of Man," also asserts, "I am the first and the last" (1:17; 22:13). Further, the singular pronoun "he" simultaneously refers to two divine persons: to God the Father, "our Lord," and also to Jesus Christ, "his Messiah." John of Patmos writes, "The kingdom of the world has become the kingdom of our Lord and of his Messiah, and *he* [the Almighty and the Messiah] will reign forever and ever" (11:15; italics added).

Yet the one God is also the divine "we." As we've noted, Revelation's opening salutation is threefold, or triune: "Grace . . . from *him who is* . . . , and from *the seven spirits* . . . , and from *Jesus Christ*" (Rev 1:4; italics added). Also, John of Patmos attests that he glimpsed the Almighty, the "one seated on the throne," who "looks like jasper and carnelian" (4:3), and that on the divine throne was also the "Lamb standing as if it had been slaughtered" (5:6). Further, emanating from the Almighty and also from the Lamb is the Holy Spirit, "the seven spirits of God" (4:5; 5:6). Finally, John conveys the three divine persons in the image of "the water of life, bright as crystal, flowing from the throne of God and of the Lamb" (22:1). In sum, God is the one Being of the Almighty, the Lamb, and the water of life.

Finally, God is the divine self-agent as well as the divine "I" and the divine "we." Indeed, each of the divine persons exercises this agency. The Almighty declares, "To the thirsty I will give water as a gift from the spring of the water of life. Those who conquer will inherit these things, and I will be their God and they will be my children" (Rev 21:6-7). Further, the Lamb "will guide" God's people "to springs of the water of life, and God will wipe away every tear from their eyes" (7:17). Finally, the Holy Spirit acts on our behalf. The Spirit gives John of Patmos his visions (1:10; 4:2) and his wisdom for the seven churches (e.g., 2:7, 11, 17). Also, the Spirit is "flowing from the throne of God and of the Lamb" (21:6). Finally, John attests, "The Spirit and the bride say, 'Come.' . . . And let everyone who is thirsty come. Let anyone who wishes take the water of life as a gift" (22:17).

B. Union and Differentiation between God and Us

The book of Revelation witnesses to the paradox of union and differentiation not only in God but also in the relationship between God and us. On the one hand, according to John of Patmos, God invites us into the marriage of the Lamb and the holy city (Rev 19:7-9) and urges us to drink the water of life so that we become united with the tree of life (2:7; 22:2, 14). In other words, the Almighty desires to draws us into the divine union of love in Jesus Christ through the Holy Spirit.

On the other hand, Revelation also attests that as God draws human persons into the divine union, God also empowers them to become individuated, to attain their distinct identities as God envisions them. This personal differentiation occurred among the "seven churches" to which John of Patmos writes his seven letters. Each of these Christian communities had its own communal personality, its own strengths, and its own tensions as it faced persecution. Moreover, according to John of Patmos, the people surrounding God stand apart from the divine throne and are also differentiated among themselves. These people include the "twenty-four elders," that is, the twelve apostles and the twelve representatives of Israel's twelve tribes (Rev 4:4), as well as the

Christian martyrs (6:9), the "one hundred and forty-four thousand" members of the twelve tribes of İsrael (7:4), and "a great multitude . . . from every nation, race, people, and tongue" (7:9). Entering into the divine union of agape generates not uniformity but diversity; it enables human persons as individuals and communities to become God's treasure, God's pearls "of great value" (Matt 13:44-46).

That our union with God paradoxically nurtures our singular personal identities in relation to God is also affirmed elsewhere in the New Testament. According to the gospels of Mark, Matthew, Luke, and John and to the Acts of the Apostles, Jesus Christ nurtured the personal wholeness, the *salus*, of each person who entered into relationship with him.

St. Peter is initially one indistinct fisherman among others on the Sea of Galilee (Mark 1:16). Yet as he shares in Jesus' life and ministry, Peter gradually matures into his role as the disciples' leader. For example, he takes a big step forward at Caesarea Philippi when he attests that Jesus is "the Christ" (8:27-29). But in Jerusalem Peter backslides as he falls asleep in the Garden of Gethsemane and subsequently denies his ties with Jesus (14:29-72). However, after Peter meets the risen Christ (1 Cor 15:5) and is filled with the Holy Spirit (Acts 2:1-4), he becomes prudent, articulate, and courageous. He holds his ground before irate Jewish authorities, the harsh Roman officials, and the assertive Jewish Christians (led by the apostle James) who want to require that Gentile Christians adhere to Jewish religious laws such as circumcision (Acts 15:5). In sum, Peter's growing union with Christ results in his personal individuation. He becomes an "I," a self-confident subject intent on witnessing to Christ and God's kingdom. Simultaneously, he develops into a "we," a full participant in as well as the primary leader of the nascent Christian community. Further, Peter emerges as a "doer," a self-agent who unites Jewish Christians and Gentile Christians in the early church. As a result of his personal integration, he eventually accepts death by crucifixion rather than back away from his true self and his vocation.

The New Testament also contains numerous brief accounts of women who attained personal individuation as they interrelated with the Lord Jesus. For example, it recounts how the Samaritan woman's encounter with Christ at Jacob's well led to her new self-confidence and self-esteem and hence her new sense of being an "I." It also tells of her new self-agency as she proclaims the Good News about Jesus to the other villagers. Further, the account reports her new "we," that is, her being in relationship with her neighbors (John 4:1-42). In this same vein, the gospels attest to the personal integrity of Mary Magdalene. During Jesus' last hours, Mary Magdalene is the subject, the "I," who has the strength and courage to remain near Jesus as he dies on the cross. Moreover, she shows herself as the interpersonal being, the "we," whose friendship with Jesus is so strong that, after his dying and rising, she is the one to whom Jesus appears at the empty tomb (John 20:14-17; Matt 28:9-10). As a result of her encounter with Christ, Mary Magdalene becomes the bold self-agent, the "doer," who publicly witnesses to Jesus' resurrection from the dead (John 20:18; Matt 28:10).

In sum, Jesus Christ through the Spirit unites us with God and simultaneously frees us to realize our God-given personal identities. He is the tree of life, the vine, to whom we are united and with whom we bear much fruit as we are nourished by the water of life, the Holy Spirit. Or, to change images, the Lamb has wed us, the holy city, through the Holy Spirit, and the Lamb has delivered us from the power of evil and death so that we may attain our personal and communal individuality. Thus, we can look forward to the day when we shall stand within the heavenly choir and add our voices to creation's chorus in singing praise and thanks to God (Rev 5:13). Thus, we may now live with the hope that our names will be inscribed in Jerusalem among "the names of the twelve tribes of the Israelites" and among "the twelve names of the twelve apostles of the Lamb" (21:12, 14).

In 1961 Thomas Merton discussed the paradox of our union and differentiation in Christ through the Spirit. The Trappist monk wrote, "In order to know and love God as He is, we must have God dwelling in us in a new way, not only in His creative power but in His mercy, not only in His greatness but in His littleness." When we permit God to come into our lives, we live within the triune or tripersonal mystery. "The Father, dwelling in the depths of all things and in my own depths, communicates to me His Word and His Spirit. Receiving them I am drawn into His own life and know God in His own Love, being one with Him in His own Son."[5] God does not, however, overwhelm us and stifle our individuality. Rather, God creates us as treasures buried in the field that God calls us to purchase for ourselves (Matt 13:44-45). Indeed, God fashions us as jewels to be raised "from the bottom of the sea."

III. Grafted on to the Tree of Life

Throughout this chapter, we have employed Václav Havel's description of his religious experience in 1980 to give us entry into the divine-
human encounter at the heart of the book of Revelation. Although
most of us are not afforded a transcendent vision akin to the divine
encounters of Václav Havel and of John of Patmos, we are surely graced
with more ordinary forms of religious experience. As Christians, we
believe that the Lord Jesus, alive in the Spirit, meets us in the church,
specifically in the sacraments, the proclamation of the Word, church
teachings, the community of believers, and our assistance to people
in need. Yet we also hold that we can encounter Christ in the Spirit
in our day-to-day lives. But what are these ordinary meeting places?
According to the Bible and the Christian tradition, they are the foundational human experiences that we celebrate at Christmas and Easter.

A. *Christmas: The Humanity of Christ and Ourselves*

Jesus Christ, alive in the Spirit, encounters us today in our humanity, that is, in our bodies, sexuality, emotions, minds, personal talents,
consciences, and interpersonal relationships. As we increasingly know
and accept our true selves, we affirm our God-given personal identities as well as God's Word and the Spirit in our lives. In particular, at
Christmas we give thanks and praise for Wisdom becoming a human
being in Jesus Christ and hence assuming our humanity.

The Second Vatican Council accentuated the saving significance of
the incarnation—celebrated at Christmas—in its Pastoral Constitution
on the Church in the Modern World, *Gaudium et Spes*, no. 22. In a
statement concerning Christ, "the new Adam," the council reiterated
the church's doctrine of Chalcedon (AD 451) that when the Word
became flesh (John 1:14), our human nature "was assumed, not ab-
sorbed, in him." God's Son did not obliterate our humanity but made
it sacred. In Vatican II's words, in Jesus Christ our human nature "has
been raised in us also to a dignity beyond compare." In other words, our
very humanity is now a potential sacrament in which we may receive
God's gift of our personal wholeness. Vatican II put it this way: "For,
by his incarnation, he, the Son of God, has in a certain way united
himself with each individual" (GS 22).

These powerful words call to mind what Jesus and Paul taught about
our God-given gifts. Jesus directed his followers, "Let your light shine

before others, so that they may see your good works and give glory to your Father in heaven" (Matt 5:16). Further, Jesus spoke of the kingdom of God, including each person's identity before God, being "a treasure hidden in a field, which someone found and hid. Then in his joy he goes and sells all that he has and buys that field" (13:44). So too, we are called by God to discover and purchase God's treasure, our very selves. Similarly, in the parable of the talents (25:14-30), Jesus praised those who use their God-given abilities in creative ways for the well-being of other people. In other words, having received from God our unique set of gifts, each of us meets God's Word and Spirit within us as we know, accept, develop, and employ our talents for the *salus* of others and of creation—in other words, for God's kingdom. After all, this process is the activity of the Spirit grafting us on to the tree of life, Christ. Speaking to this point, Paul wrote, "Now we have received not the spirit of the world, but the Spirit that is from God, so that we may understand the gifts bestowed on us by God" (1 Cor 2:12).

Consider again Thomas Merton's words of 1961. Reflecting on our personal existence in relation to the incarnation, he wrote, "God utters me like a word containing a partial thought of Himself." That is, God speaks within each of us, calling us into being, into the singular persons whom God intends. We cannot, however, fully grasp this mystery. "A word will never be able to comprehend the voice that utters it. But if I am true to the concept that God utters in me, if I am true to the thought of Him I was meant to embody, I shall be full of His actuality and find Him everywhere in myself, and find myself nowhere. I shall be lost in Him; that is, I shall find myself. I shall be 'saved.'"[6]

Independent of Merton, Romano Guardini expressed a similar insight in 1964 when he noted that God speaks the Word in each human being at birth. "Everything that then occurs in the person's life is somehow related to the realization of this word. A human life is an elucidation and fulfillment of the divine word which influences all aspects of this life. This word is spoken to each human being. It understands each of us and comes into harmony with us. This word is perhaps the basis on which God will eventually judge each human being."[7] In sum, Guardini affirmed that we can meet the living Christ through the Spirit in ourselves, specifically in our deepest desires, our abilities, our interpersonal relationships, and even our limitations and failures.

B. Easter: The Death and Resurrection of Christ and Ourselves

A second meeting place for our encounter with Christ in the Spirit is a situation of disruption and even collapse. When we undergo loss (e.g., coping with terminal illness, unemployment, or divorce), we are tempted "to throw in the towel," to allow a sense of defeat and sadness to get the best of us (see chap. 3). Yet belief in the paschal mystery—that is, in Jesus Christ's life, death, resurrection, and future coming, or Parousia, which we celebrate at Easter—reveals that we need not settle for a dead end, for dying in a cold, dark place. Rather, we can hope in God. Trusting in God, we can anticipate a new beginning, especially when we see ourselves moving from loss to active waiting and then from active waiting to discovery—in other words, when we see that we're moving from death to resurrection in Christ through the Spirit.

In *Gaudium et Spes* the Second Vatican Council shed fresh light on Easter. It affirmed that all people may share in the paschal mystery. Through their baptisms and participation in the church, Christians are oriented to Christ in the Spirit amid life's disappointments and losses. "The Christian is certainly bound both by need and by duty to struggle with evil through many afflictions and to suffer death; but, as one who has been made a partner in the paschal mystery, and as one who has been configured to the death of Christ, [the Christian] will go forward, strengthened by hope to the resurrection" (GS 22).

At the same time, all people may also live in the paschal mystery: "All this holds true not only for Christians but also for all people of good will in whose hearts grace is active invisibly. . . . The Holy Spirit offers to all the possibility of being made partners, in a way known to God, in the paschal mystery" (GS 22). Indeed, Christ through the Holy Spirit reaches out to all people. "Constituted Lord by his resurrection and given all authority in heaven and on earth, Christ is now at work in human hearts by the power of his Spirit" (GS 22; cf. GS 38).

Vatican II's insight into our participation in the paschal mystery has a firm foundation in the teachings of the Lord Jesus and St. Paul. Jesus himself reiterated that our experiences of loss, even of dying, can become moments of grace, moments of receiving God's gift of salvation. In Jesus' words, "Those who want to save their life will lose it, and those who lose their life for my sake, and for the sake of the gospel, will save it" (Mark 8:35). According to St. John, Jesus compared our loss, our waiting, and our finding to a seed's burial in the ground, its apparent death, and then its animation to new life: "Very truly, I tell you, unless a grain of wheat falls into the earth and dies, it remains just a single grain; but if it dies, it bears much fruit" (John 12:24).

St. Paul stresses the dynamism of losing, searching, and finding ourselves in Jesus Christ through the Spirit. Concerning our literal deaths, Paul writes: "So it is with the resurrection of the dead. What is sown is perishable, what is raised is imperishable. . . . It is sown a physical body, it is raised a spiritual body" (1 Cor 15:42-44). Further, Paul applies his words on disruption, hope, and new life to our figurative deaths as well as to our literal deaths. He writes, "We are afflicted in every way, but not crushed; . . . struck down, but not destroyed; always carrying in the body the death of Jesus, so that the life of Jesus may also be made visible in our bodies" (2 Cor 4:8-10). Reiterating this conviction, Paul declares, "If we have been united with him [Christ] in a death like his, we will certainly be united with him in a resurrection like his" (Rom 6:5; see Phil 3:10-11; 2 Tim 2:11-12).

Independent of each other, Thomas Merton and Romano Guardini wrote that the Lord Jesus through the Spirit walks with us as we cope with life's hardships and apparent dead ends. According to Merton, we must await God's strength and counsel when we are "beaten down." In his words, the person "who lets God lead him peacefully through the wilderness, and desires no other support or guidance than that of pure faith and trust in God alone, will be brought to the Promised Land." Moreover, after we acknowledge one experience of God being with us as we suffer a loss, seek a way forward, and eventually receive a new start, then we can trust anew in Christ and the Spirit whenever we face another loss. A person may develop "a habitual, comforting, obscure and mysterious awareness of his God, present and acting in all the events of his life."[8] In other words, as we learn during our figurative deaths how to undergo collapse, waiting, and discovering, we can develop the faith and skills for coping with our literal deaths.

Speaking of this same truth, Guardini observed that the Lord Jesus chooses to be with us in our "dark valleys," especially in our literal deaths, which are "the darkest valley" (cf. Ps 23:4). Christ, the Good Shepherd (John 10), in the Spirit walks with us through those "places" where we are most alone. As we are dealing with loss, especially our dying or the dying of a loved one, we may stand in a "space" that other people cannot enter—"not our father, not our mother, not our brother or sister, neither our loved ones nor our friends." We may feel isolated in this cold, dark realm. "But Christ is there. He alone is there because, after having lived for us, he has died for us, and, rising from the tomb, he has conquered death. In death, he has established a mysterious bond between himself and us. . . . Whenever a believer undergoes death, Christ undergoes it, too."[9]

John of Patmos in AD 95 and Václav Havel in 1980 found themselves imprisoned and yet received God's new life, *salus*. Moreover, both of them expressed this religious experience through the image of a flourishing tree. Upon reflection, Havel viewed the tree as a symbol of "Being" at the heart of human existence and judged that in his encounter with "Being" he was "struck by love." In Revelation, John of Patmos employed the biblical images of the tree of life and the water of life in order to express how the Lord Jesus and the Spirit meet us in our human nature and also in our hardships. According to John, our encounters with Christ in the Spirit assure us of the Father's promise: "I am the Alpha and the Omega, the beginning and the end. To the thirsty I will give water as a gift from the spring of the water of life. Those who conquer will inherit these things, and I will be their God and they will be my children" (Rev 21:6-7).

IV. Living in the Triune God

By AD 200, Christians were commonly making the sign of the cross. At first, they traced it on their foreheads with the right thumb. But they eventually extended this symbolic action from the forehead to the chest and from shoulder to shoulder. Today, in the Western church, the right hand moves from left to right, whereas in the Eastern church the cross stroke is from right to left. In both cases, all believers accompany the action of their hands with the words "In the name of the Father and of the Son and of the Holy Spirit." Thus, in making the sign of the cross, Christians declare that human beings receive God's gift of salvation through their participation in the mystery of the triune God. In particular, they declare that we are saved as we are united through the Holy Spirit in Jesus Christ's incarnation, life, death, resurrection, and Parousia.

The church now formally professes its belief in the triune God in its Nicene Creed, the Creed that was formulated by the Council of Nicea (AD 325) and enlarged by the Council of Constantinople (AD 381). This confession of faith, which we recite at Mass on Sundays, emerged out of the witness of the first Christians. In AD 57 St. Paul concluded his second letter to the Christians at Corinth with this blessing: "The grace of the Lord Jesus Christ, the love of God, and the communion of the Holy Spirit be with all of you" (2 Cor 13:13; see 1 Cor 8:6). In AD 85 St. Matthew drew on an oral tradition when he ended his gospel with Christ instructing his disciples, "Go therefore and make disciples of all nations, baptizing them in the name of the Father and of the Son and of the Holy Spirit" (Matt 28:19). Further, in AD 90 the evangelist St. John wrote that Jesus concluded his "farewell discourse" with this promise: "When the Advocate comes, whom I will send to you from the Father, the Spirit of truth who comes from the Father, he will testify on my behalf" (John 15:26). Finally, as we have seen, John of Patmos in AD 95 attested to the triune God in his image of God enthroned as the Almighty, the Lamb, and the water of life (Rev 22:1).

Drawing on the book of Revelation, the Second Vatican Council viewed creation and history in relation to our becoming united with the triune God. In *Gaudium et Spes*, no. 45, the council acknowledged that Jesus Christ is God's Son and the Savior of all people: "*The Word* of God, through whom all things were made, was made flesh, so that as a perfect man he could save all women and men and sum up all things in himself. The Lord is the goal of history, the focal point of the desires of history and civilization, the center of humanity, the joy of all hearts, and the fulfillment of all aspirations" (italics added). Yet the Lord Jesus, the Lamb, does not operate alone but lives and acts among us in relation to the Almighty: "It is [Christ] whom *the Father* raised from the dead, exalted and placed at his right hand, constituting him judge of the living and the dead" (italics added). At the same time, the Holy Spirit who flows as the water of life from the Father and the Son inspires and guides us in our salvation: "Animated and drawn together in his *Spirit* we press onwards on our journey towards the consummation of history which fully corresponds to the plan of his love: 'to unite all things in [Jesus Christ], things in heaven and things on earth' (Eph 1:10)" (italics added). In conclusion, Vatican II urged all Christians to keep in mind the Lord's promise at the end of the book of Revelation: "See, I am coming soon. . . . I am the Alpha and the Omega, the first and the last, the beginning and the end" (Rev 22:12-13).

In light of the Second Vatican Council's testimony, as well as the biblical witness to the mystery of our lives in the triune God, what are we declaring when we make the sign of the cross?

As we make the sign of the cross, we declare that we are God's works in progress and that our life stories receive their full significance only in relation to God's story of salvation in creation and history. Calling to mind the God who is the Almighty, the Lamb, and the water of life can awaken in us the awareness that we live between the "already" and the "not yet." On the one hand, insofar as we are living in Christ through the Spirit, we are increasingly affirming ourselves as embodied persons, each of whom is becoming an "I," a "we," and a "doer." On the other hand, insofar as we have not yet fully become one with Christ through the Spirit, we are painfully conscious of our alienation from ourselves, from other people, from the earth, and most importantly from the triune God. We live, therefore, in the interim between our partial *salus* and the completion of our salvation in God's eternal life.

In 1927 Romano Guardini wrote that all of us should be more deliberate about making the sign of the cross. Instead of moving our hand quickly in a small circle, we should "do it slowly, grandly, from the forehead to the chest, from one shoulder to the other." As we do this, we may sense how God's salvation "completely encircles" us. If a person will allow it, the sign of the cross "pulls you together, consecrates you, and sanctifies you." Why? "Through the cross, Christ sanctifies every human being, entirely, to the last fiber of his or her being." The sign of the cross is, therefore, our acknowledgement of God's gift of our personal wholeness in union with Christ through the Holy Spirit. "In this sign, all will be strengthened, dedicated, consecrated in the power of Christ, in the name of the triune God."[10]

Since we make our life journeys as God's works in progress, we benefit when we make the sign of the cross with reverence. For whenever we bless ourselves in this ancient ritual, we give witness to God's gift of *salus*, of God's wellness, which we are now receiving and which we shall fully embrace when we join with God's people around the heavenly throne of the Almighty, the Lamb, and the water of life. Therefore, let us give thanks and praise to the God of our salvation as we pray, "In the name of the Father and of the Son and of the Holy Spirit."

Notes

Preface

1. See Daniel J. Harrington, *How Do Catholics Read the Bible?* (Lanham, MD: Rowman & Littlefield, 2005), 102–6.

Chapter 1 (pages 1–20)

1. Thomas Merton, *New Seeds of Contemplation* (Boston: Shambhala, 2003 [1961]), 39–40.
2. Ibid., 39.
3. Hannah Arendt, *The Human Condition* (Chicago: Chicago University Press, 1958), 186.

Chapter 2 (pages 21–40)

1. Thomas Merton, *New Seeds of Contemplation* (Boston: Shambhala, 2003 [1961]), 36.
2. John Henry Cardinal Newman, *An Essay in Aid of a Grammar of Ascent* (Notre Dame, IN: University of Notre Dame Press, 1979 [1870]), 157–72.
3. Merton, *New Seeds of Contemplation*, 37–38.

Chapter 3 (pages 41–60)

1. *Catechism of the Catholic Church*, 2nd ed. (Vatican City: Libreria Editrice Vaticana, 1994), no. 1431.
2. See ibid., no. 1428.
3. Thomas Merton, *New Seeds of Contemplation* (Boston: Shambhala, 2003 [1961]), 49.
4. Dag Hammarskjold, *Markings*, trans. Leif Sjöberg and W. H. Auden (New York: Alfred A. Knopf, 1964), 205.

5. Rainer Maria Rilke, *Letters to a Young Poet*, trans. Mark Harman (Cambridge, MA: Harvard University Press, 2011), 71.

Chapter 4 (pages 61–80)

1. Karl Rahner, *Theological Investigations*, trans. Edward Quinn, vol. 19 (New York: Crossroad, 1983), 208.

2. Sidney Callahan, *Created for Joy: A Christian View of Suffering* (New York: Crossroad, 2007), 9.

3. See C. S. Lewis, *The Screwtape Letters* (San Francisco: HarperSanFrancisco, 2001 [1942]).

4. Doris Kearns Goodwin, *Team of Rivals* (New York: Simon and Schuster, 2006), 49.

5. Joseph Berger, "A Witness to Evil: Eliezer Wiesel," *The New York Times* (October 15, 1986), 10.

6. See Michael D. Coogan, *The Old Testament* (New York: Oxford University Press, 2006), 461–64.

7. Robert A. Krieg, ed. and trans., *Romano Guardini: Spiritual Writings* (Maryknoll, NY: Orbis Books, 2005), 84.

8. Ibid., 85.

Chapter 5 (pages 81–100)

1. J. R. R. Tolkien, "On Fairy Stories," in *Tree and Leaf* (Boston: Houghton Mifflin Company, 1965), 3–84, esp. 67–68.

2. Ibid., 72.

3. *The Oxford English Dictionary*, 2nd ed. (1989).

4. *Phaedo*, trans. Hugh Tredennick, in *The Collected Dialogues of Plato, Including the Letters*, ed. Edith Hamilton and Huntington Cairns (Princeton, NJ: Princeton University Press, 1963), 88, 95.

5. Jon D. Levenson, *Resurrection and the Restoration of Israel* (New Haven, CT: Yale University Press, 2006), 20.

6. *Republic*, trans. Paul Shorey, in *The Collected Dialogues of Plato, Including the Letters*, 609.

7. Jon Levenson, *Resurrection and the Restoration of Israel*, 106.

8. *The Old Testament Pseudepigrapha*, vol. 1, ed. James H. Charlesworth (Garden City, NY: Doubleday, 1983), 13–29.

9. Ibid., 34.

Chapter 6 (pages 101–20)

1. Karl Rahner, *The Love of Jesus and the Love of Neighbor*, trans. Robert Barr (New York: Crossroad, 1983), 22.

Chapter 7 (pages 121–40)

1. See John Howard Griffin, *Scattered Shadows* (Maryknoll, NY: Orbis Books, 2004).

2. See Randy Pausch, *The Last Lecture* (New York: Hyperion: 2008).

Chapter 8 (pages 141–59)

1. See Richard Bauckham, *The Theology of the Book of Revelation* (Cambridge: Cambridge University Press, 1993).

2. Václav Havel, *Letters to Olga, June 1979–September 1982*, trans. Paul Wilson (New York: Alfred A. Knopf, 1988), 331.

3. Ibid., 331–32.

4. Ibid., 332.

5. Thomas Merton, *New Seeds of Contemplation* (Boston: Shambhala, 2003 [1961]), 42.

6. Ibid., 39.

7. Robert A. Krieg, ed. and trans., *Romano Guardini: Spiritual Writings* (Maryknoll, NY: Orbis Books, 2005), 48.

8. Merton, *New Seeds of Contemplation*, 243.

9. Krieg, *Romano Guardini: Spiritual Writings*, 136.

10. Ibid., 141–42.

Index